Weather and Climate Inventory
National Park Service
Pacific Island Network

Natural Resource Technical Report NPS/PACN/NRTR—2006/003
WRCC Report 06-04

Christopher A. Davey, Kelly T. Redmond, and David B. Simeral
Western Regional Climate Center
Desert Research Institute
2215 Raggio Parkway
Reno, Nevada 89512-1095

August 2006

U.S. Department of the Interior
National Park Service
Natural Resource Program Center
Fort Collins, Colorado

The Natural Resource Publication series addresses natural resource topics that are of interest and applicability to a broad readership in the National Park Service and to others in the management of natural resources, including the scientific community, the public, and the National Park Service conservation and environmental constituencies. Manuscripts are peer-reviewed to ensure that the information is scientifically credible, technically accurate, appropriately written for the intended audience, and designed and published in a professional manner.

The Natural Resource Technical Reports series is used to disseminate the peer-reviewed results of scientific studies in the physical, biological, and social sciences for both the advancement of science and the achievement of the National Park Service's mission. The reports provide contributors with a forum for displaying comprehensive data that are often deleted from journals because of page limitations. Current examples of such reports include the results of research that addresses natural resource management issues; natural resource inventory and monitoring activities; resource assessment reports; scientific literature reviews; and peer reviewed proceedings of technical workshops, conferences, or symposia.

Views and conclusions in this report are those of the authors and do not necessarily reflect policies of the National Park Service. Mention of trade names or commercial products does not constitute endorsement or recommendation for use by the National Park Service.

Printed copies of reports in these series may be produced in a limited quantity and they are only available as long as the supply lasts. This report is also available from the Natural Resource Publications Management website (http://www.nature.nps.gov/publications/NRPM) on the Internet or by sending a request to the address on the back cover.

Please cite this publication as follows:

Davey, C. A., K. T. Redmond, and D. B. Simeral. 2006. Weather and Climate Inventory, National Park Service, Pacific Island Network. Natural Resource Technical Report NPS/PACN/NRTR—2006/003. National Park Service, Fort Collins, Colorado.

NPS/PACN/NRTR—2006/003, August 2006

Table of Contents

Table of Contents (continued)

Figures

Tables

Appendixes

Acronyms

AASC	American Association of State Climatologists
ACIS	Applied Climate Information System
ALKA	Ala Kahakai National Historic Trail
AMME	American Memorial Park
ASOS	Automated Surface Observing System
AWOS	Automated Weather Observing System
BLM	Bureau of Land Management
CASTNet	Clean Air Status and Trends Network
COOP	Cooperative Observer Program
CRN	Climate Reference Network
CWOP	Citizen Weather Observer Program
DFIR	Double-Fence Intercomparison Reference
DST	daylight savings time
ENSO	El Niño Southern Oscillation
EPA	Environmental Protection Agency
FAA	Federal Aviation Administration
FIPS	Federal Information Processing Standards
GMT	Greenwich Mean Time
GOES	Geostationary Operational Environmental Satellite
GPMP	Gaseous Pollutant Monitoring Program
GPS	Global Positioning System
GPSMET	The University Center for Atmospheric Research GPS/MET Experiment
HALE	Haleakala National Park
HaleNet	Haleakala Climate Network
HAVO	Hawaii Volcanoes National Park
I&M	NPS Inventory and Monitoring Program
KAHO	Kaloko-Honokohau National Historical Park
KALA	Kalaupapa National Historical Park
LST	local standard time
NADP	National Atmospheric Deposition Program
NASA	National Aeronautics and Space Administration
NCDC	National Climatic Data Center
NetCDF	Network Common Data Form
NOAA	National Oceanic and Atmospheric Administration
NPS	National Park Service
NPSA	National Park of American Samoa
NRCS	Natural Resources Conservation Service
NWS	National Weather Service
OBOP	NOAA Earth Systems Research Laboratory Observatory Operations Group
PACN	Pacific Island Inventory and Monitoring Network
PDO	Pacific Decadal Oscillation
PRISM	Parameter Regression on Independent Slopes Model

PUHE	Puuhokola Heiau National Historic Site
PUHO	Puuhonua o Honaunau National Historical Park
RAWS	Remote Automated Weather Station
RCC	regional climate center
SAO	Surface Airways Observations Program
Surfrad	Surface Radiation Budget Network
UCAR	University Center for Atmospheric Research
USAR	USS Arizona Memorial
USDA	U.S. Department of Agriculture
USGS	U.S. Geological Survey
UTC	Coordinated Universal Time
WAPA	War in the Pacific National Historical Park
WBAN	Weather Bureau Army Navy
WRCC	Western Regional Climate Center
WMO	World Meteorological Organization

Executive Summary

Climate is one of the primary factors that determine ecosystem characteristics. Impacts on natural systems due to global- and regional-scale climate variations are particularly pronounced in island systems, highlighting the importance of weather and climate monitoring efforts in these areas. Significant variations in elevation among the Pacific Island Inventory and Monitoring Network (PACN) park units lead to a wide diversity of climate zones that sustain diverse ecosystem types within PACN. The PACN is vulnerable to drought conditions due to limited freshwater resources. Climatic consequences of the El Niño-Southern Oscillation (ENSO) are much more pronounced in the PACN than in other parts of the world, including increased tropical cyclone frequency, increased sea surface temperatures, and extended drought conditions. Projected climate changes are likely to adversely affect many aspects of PACN ecosystems, including eradication of native species and declining coral reef health. Human-induced climate changes may further stress PACN ecosystems that are already stressed by introduction of invasive species and urban developments. Climate monitoring is also valuable for managing the cultural resources of PACN. Respect for weather and climate is common among Pacific Islanders. These weather and climate features were often honored in song and dance. Much of this rich cultural heritage may be threatened by sea level changes due to future regional- and global-scale climatic changes.

This report inventories past and present climate monitoring efforts in PACN. In the report, we provide the following information:

- Overview of broad-scale climatic factors and zones important to PACN park units.
- Inventory of weather station locations in and near PACN park units.
- Results of an inventory of metadata on each weather station, including affiliations for weather-monitoring networks, types of measurements recorded at these stations, and information about the actual measurements (length of record, etc.).
- Initial evaluation of the adequacy of coverage for existing weather stations and recommendations for improvements in monitoring weather and climate.

The tropical-marine climate of PACN provides relatively uniform temporal temperature characteristics throughout the region. There are spatial variations in temperature introduced by elevational temperature gradients that are particularly important on larger islands. In contrast to temperature, precipitation is often highly variable on the PACN, both spatially and temporally, due to influences from topography and trade winds and interannual variations caused by ENSO and other climate phenomena. This is particularly true in the park units on the Hawaiian Islands, where mean annual precipitation totals range from under 250 mm at Puukohola Heiau National Historic Site (PUHE), on the northwest shore of the island of Hawaii, to well over 6000 mm on the northeast slopes of Haleakala in Haleakala National Park (HALE), on the island of Maui. The dominant trade wind patterns in PACN lead to generally higher precipitation on the windward (east) sides of the islands. The highest elevations of the PACN islands, including portions of Hawaii Volcanoes National Park (HAVO), lie above the trade wind inversion and therefore have drier conditions relative to lower elevations. The dominant trade-wind patterns can occasionally be disrupted by tropical cyclone activity, which increases during warm ENSO phases.

Through a search of national databases and inquiries to NPS staff, we have identified 25 weather and climate stations within PACN park units. These include 23 stations in the park units of the Hawaiian Islands, one station at War in the Pacific National Historical Park (WAPA), and one station in the National Park of American Samoa (NPSA). Many of the smaller park units on the Hawaiian Islands have numerous manual and automated weather and climate stations located nearby. Most of the manual stations in PACN are associated with the National Weather Service Cooperative Observer Program (COOP) and most of these sites only measure precipitation. The majority of automated stations in PACN are associated with either the Remote Automated Weather Station network (RAWS) or the Surface Airways Observation Network (SAO). Metadata and data records for most of the weather and climate stations identified within the PACN region are sufficiently complete and of satisfactory quality. The primary exceptions to this are for stations in the Citizen Weather Observer Program (CWOP) and GPS/MET networks.

The small areal extent of the islands in PACN limits the expansion of existing land-based weather and climate monitoring networks. Therefore, it is important that any active stations be maintained to ensure continuing reliable observations, as the climate records available from such stations are useful in tracking global-scale climatic changes. In regions with high gradients in climate characteristics, any small moves can more readily introduce artificial climate changes. Also, it may be beneficial to NPS climate monitoring efforts to re-activate those stations that have recently become inactive. These efforts are particularly important at sites such as those on or near the summit of Mauna Loa, which is a location widely noted for ongoing long-term climate monitoring efforts. The NPS can play a role in these efforts by actively participating with local officials and agencies that are responsible for these currently-operating stations.

The current absence of near-real-time stations at or near Puuhonua o Honaunau National Historical Park (PUHO) suggests that it may be advantageous to work with the RAWS network to install a station at lower elevations on the west slopes of Mauna Loa. This would not only provide real-time weather conditions for PUHO but could also benefit local fire management efforts.

Similarly, the present lack of any real-time weather observations on the American Samoa Manua Group islands may be detrimental for management of the National Park of American Samoa park units that are on these islands. A possible solution would be to encourage the installation of a SAO site or a RAWS site at Tau Airport, to complement the existing COOP station. In the meantime, it is important to support the continuation of the active manual stations on the Manua Group islands, as they are currently the only source of weather observations for those islands. A RAWS station is planned for installation at WAPA. We recommend elevated sites to maximize exposure in all directions. Potential sites include Mt. Chachao / Mt. Tenjo, Mt. Alifon and Fonte Plateau.

Acknowledgements

This work was supported and completed under Task Agreement H8R07010001 with the Great Basin Cooperative Ecosystem Studies Unit. We would like to acknowledge very helpful assistance from various National Park Service personnel associated with the Pacific Island Inventory and Monitoring Network. Particular thanks are extended to Leslie HaySmith, Fritz Klasner, Karin Schlappa, John Gross, and Margaret Beer. Grant Kelly, Heather Angeloff, and Greg McCurdy, all from the Western Regional Climate Center, also provided valuable assistance in producing this report. Portions of the work also were supported by the Western Regional Climate Center under the auspices of the National Oceanic and Atmospheric Administration.

1.0. Introduction

Weather and climate are key drivers in ecosystem structure and function. Global- and regional-scale climate variations will have a tremendous impact on natural systems (Schlesinger 1997; Jacobson et al. 2000; Bonan 2002). Long-term patterns in temperature and precipitation provide first-order constraints on potential ecosystem structure and function. Secondary constraints are realized from the intensity and duration of individual weather events and, additionally, from seasonality and inter-annual climate variability. These constraints influence the fundamental properties of ecologic systems, such as soil–water relationships, plant–soil processes, and nutrient cycling, as well as disturbance rates and intensity. These properties, in turn, influence the life-history strategies supported by a climatic regime (Neilson 1987).

Given the importance of climate, it is one of 12 basic inventories to be completed by the National Park Service (NPS) Inventory and Monitoring Program (I&M) network (I&M 2006). As primary environmental drivers for the other vital signs, weather and climate patterns present a myriad of practical and management consequences and implications for the NPS (Oakley et al. 2003). Most park units observe weather and climate elements as part of their overall mission. The lands under NPS stewardship provide many excellent locations for monitoring climatic conditions.

It is essential that park units within the Pacific Island Inventory and Monitoring Network (PACN) have an effective climate-monitoring system in place to track climate changes and to aid in management decisions relating to these changes. The primary emphasis of weather and climate monitoring in the PACN is to document or define 'normal' climatic conditions, including spatial and temporal variability. Knowledge of these conditions can then be used to evaluate the effects of weather and climate on other natural resources. Further objectives for climate- and weather-monitoring in the PACN are as follows (HaySmith et al. 2005; Schlappa 2005):

A. Identify the range of variation in weather patterns across the PACN.
B. Identify and monitor early indicators of climate change, such as climate forcing events.

More specific climate-monitoring questions that have been raised by the PACN include the following (HaySmith et al. 2005; Schlappa 2005):

A. What are the ranges of average (statistical mean) conditions for monthly, yearly, and seasonal values of core weather parameters (relative humidity, temperature, precipitation, wind speed and direction, cloud cover) on a park-wide, island-wide, network-wide spatial scale?
B. What are the trends for core climate parameters on park-wide, island-wide and network-wide scales?
C. What are the long-term trends for other parameters (selected based on site-specific needs) such as, trade wind inversion, lifting condensation level, ultraviolet radiation, cloud immersion time?

D. What are the limits of extreme conditions for the core weather parameters?
E. What is the frequency, spatial extent, and duration of extreme weather events such as droughts, tropical cyclones, El Nino cycles, PDO, changes in predominant wind patterns?

Realization of these objectives will help in the evaluation of climate effects on other natural resources being monitored by the PACN.

The purpose of this report is to determine the current status of weather and climate monitoring within the PACN (Figure 1.1, Table 1.1), which has been hampered by a lack of weather and climate data within many PACN park units (HaySmith et al. 2005). In this report, we provide the following informational elements:

- Overview of broad-scale climatic factors and zones important to PACN park units.
- Inventory of locations for all weather stations in and near PACN park units that are relevant to the NPS I&M networks.
- Results of metadata inventory for each station, including weather-monitoring network affiliations, types of recorded measurements, and information about actual measurements (length of record, etc.).
- Initial evaluation of the adequacy of coverage for existing weather stations and recommendations for improvements in monitoring weather and climate.

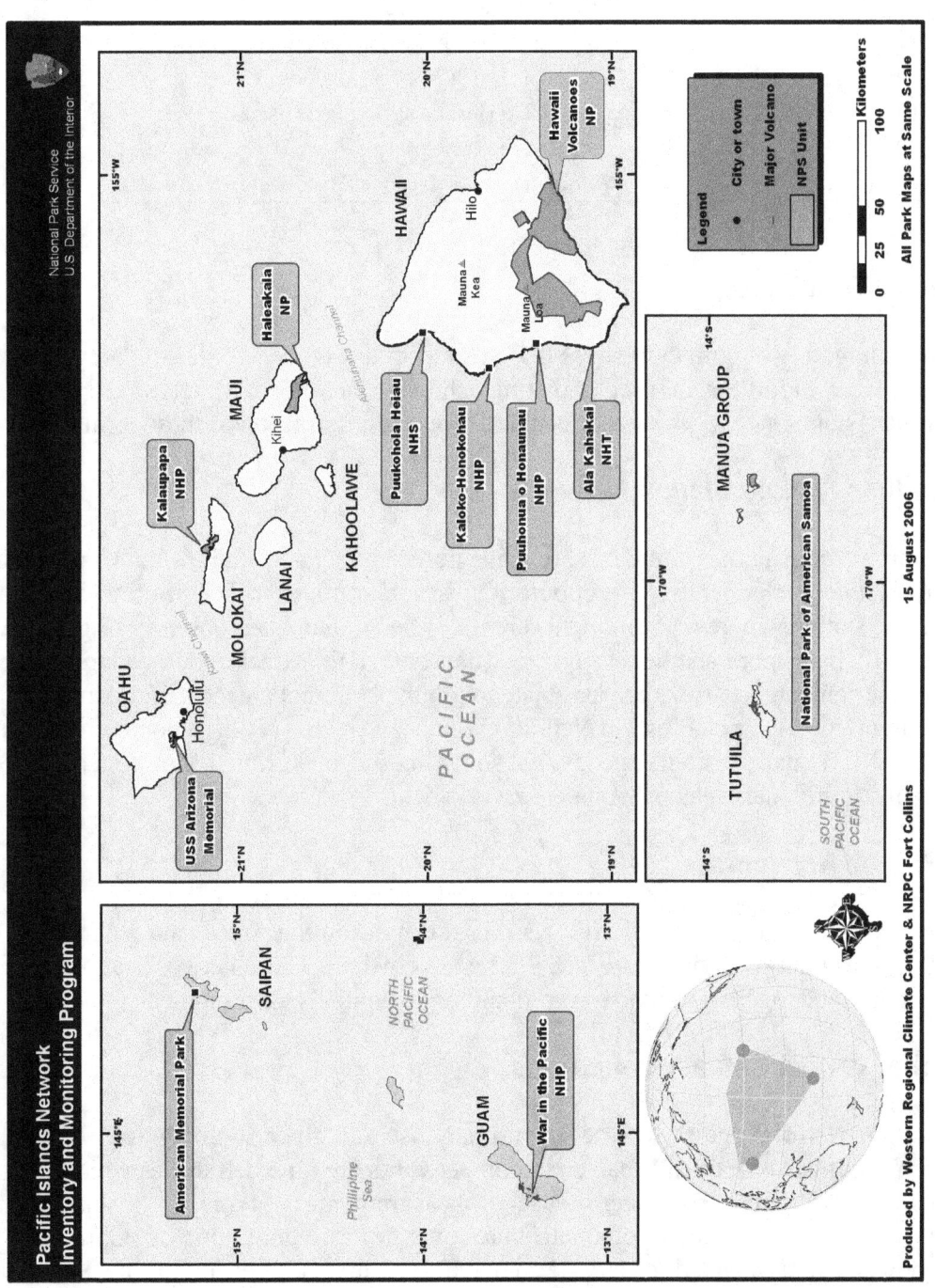

Figure 1.1. Map of the Pacific Island Inventory and Monitoring Network (PACN).

3

Table 1.1. Park units in the PACN.

Acronym	Name
ALKA	Ala Kahakai National Historic Trail
AMME	American Memorial Park
HALE	Haleakala National Park
HAVO	Hawaii Volcanoes National Park
KAHO	Kaloko-Honokohau National Historical Park
KALA	Kalaupapa National Historical Park
NPSA	National Park of American Samoa
PUHE	Puukohola Heiau National Historic Site
PUHO	Puuhonoa o Honaunau National Historical Park
USAR	USS Arizona Memorial
WAPA	War in the Pacific National Historical Park

1.1. Network Terminology

Before proceeding, it is important to stress that this report discusses the idea of "networks" in two different ways. Modifiers are used to distinguish between NPS I&M networks and weather/climate station networks. See Appendix B for a full definition of these terms.

1.1.1. Weather/Climate Station Networks

Most weather and climate measurements are made not from isolated stations but from stations that are part of a network operating in support of a particular mission. The limiting case is a network of one station, where measurements are made by an interested observer or group. Larger networks usually have more and better inventory data and station-tracking procedures. Some national weather/climate networks are associated with the National Oceanic and Atmospheric Administration (NOAA), including the National Weather Service (NWS) Cooperative Observer Program (COOP). Usually a single agency, but sometimes a consortium of interested parties, will jointly support a particular weather/climate network.

1.1.2. NPS I&M Networks

Within the NPS, the system for monitoring various attributes in the participating park units (about 280–290 in total) is divided into 32 NPS I&M networks. These networks are collections of park units grouped together around a common theme, typically geographical.

1.2. Weather versus Climate Definitions

It is also important to distinguish whether the primary use of a given station is for weather purposes or for climate purposes. Weather station networks are intended for near-real-time usage, where the precise circumstances of a set of measurements are typically less important. In these cases, changes in exposure or other attributes over time are not as critical. Climate networks, however, are intended for long-term tracking of atmospheric conditions. Siting and exposure are critical factors for climate networks, and it is vitally important that the observational circumstances remain essentially unchanged over the duration of the station record. Some climate networks can be considered hybrids of weather/climate networks. These hybrid climate networks can supply information on a short-term "weather" time scale and a longer-term "climate" time scale.

In this report, "weather" generally refers to current (or near-real-time) atmospheric conditions, while "climate" is defined as the complete ensemble of statistical descriptors for temporal and spatial properties of atmospheric behavior (see Appendix B). Climate and weather phenomena shade gradually into each other and are ultimately inseparable.

1.3. Purpose of Measurements

Inventorying and monitoring climate activities should be based on a set of guiding fundamental principles. The starting point in evaluating weather/climate monitoring programs begins with asking the following question:

- What is the purpose of weather and climate measurements?

Evaluation of past, present, or planned weather/climate monitoring activities must be based on the answer to this question. Within the context of the NPS, the following services constitute the main purposes for recording weather and climate observations:

- Provide measurements for real-time operational needs and early warnings of potential hazards (landslides, mudflows, washouts, fallen trees, fire conditions, aircraft and watercraft conditions, road conditions, rescue conditions, fog, restoration and remediation activities, etc.).
- Provide visitor education and aid interpretation of expected and actual conditions for visitors to use while in the park and for deciding if and when to visit the park.
- Establish engineering and design criteria for structures, roads, culverts, etc., for human comfort, safety, and economic needs.
- Monitor climate consistently over the long term to detect changes in environmental drivers affecting ecosystems, including both gradual and sudden events.
- Provide retrospective data to understand *a posteriori* changes in flora and fauna.
- Document for posterity the physical conditions in and near the park units, including mean, extreme, and variable measurements (in time and space) for all applications.

The last three items in the preceding list are pertinent primarily to the NPS I&M networks; however, all items are important to NPS operations and management. Most of the needs in this list overlap heavily. It is often impractical to operate separate-climate measuring systems that also cannot be used to meet ordinary weather needs, where there is greater emphasis on timeliness and reliability.

1.4. Design of Climate-Monitoring Programs

Determining the purposes for collecting measurements in a given weather/climate monitoring program will guide the process of identifying weather/climate stations suitable for the monitoring program. The context for making these decisions is provided in Chapter 2 where background on the PACN climate is presented. However, the design process is only one step in evaluating and designing a climate-monitoring program. This process includes the following additional steps:

- Define park and network-specific monitoring needs and objectives.
- Identify locations and data repositories of existing and historic stations.
- Acquire existing data when necessary or practical.
- Evaluate the quality of existing data.
- Evaluate the adequacy of coverage of existing stations.
- Develop a protocol for monitoring the weather and climate, including the following:
  - Standardized summaries and reports of weather/climate data.
  - Data management (quality assurance and quality control, archiving, data access, etc.).
- Develop and implement a plan for installing or modifying stations, as necessary.

Throughout the design process, there are various factors that require consideration in evaluating weather- and climate-measuring activities. Many of these factors have been summarized by Dr. Tom Karl, director of the NOAA National Climatic Data Center (NCDC), and widely distributed as the "Ten Principles for Climate Monitoring" (Karl et al. 1996; NRC 2001). These principles are presented in Appendix A, and the guidelines are embodied in many of the comments made throughout this report. The most critical factors are presented here. In addition, an overview of requirements necessary to operate a climate network is provided in Appendix C, with further discussion in Appendix E.

1.4.1. Need for Consistency

A principal goal in climate monitoring is to detect and characterize slow and sudden changes in climate through time. This is of less concern for day-to-day weather changes, but it is of paramount importance for climate variability and change. There are many ways whereby changes in techniques for making measurements, adjustments in instruments or their exposures, or seemingly innocuous changes in site characteristics can lead to apparent changes in climate. Safeguards must be in place to avoid these false sources of temporal "climate" variability if we are to draw correct inferences about climate behavior through time from archived measurements.

For climate monitoring, consistency through time is vital, counting at least as important as absolute accuracy. Sensors record only what is occurring at the sensor—this is all they can detect. It is the responsibility of station or station network managers to ensure that observations are representative of the spatial and temporal climate scales that we wish to record.

1.4.2. Metadata

Changes in instruments, site characteristics, and observing methodologies can lead to apparent changes in climate through time. It is therefore vital to document all factors that can bear on the interpretation of climate measurements and to update the information repeatedly through time. This information ("metadata," data about data) has its own history and set of quality-control issues that parallel those of the actual data. There is no single standard for the content of climate metadata, but a simple rule suffices:

- Observers should record all information that could be needed in the future to interpret observations correctly without benefit of the observers' personal recollections.

Such documentation includes notes, drawings, site forms, and photos, which can be of inestimable value if taken in the correct manner. That stated, it is not always clear to the metadata provider *what is important* for posterity and *what will be important* in the future. It is almost impossible to "over-document" a station. Station documentation is underappreciated greatly and seldom thorough enough (especially for climate purposes). Insufficient attention to this issue often lowers the present and especially future value of otherwise useful data.

The convention followed throughout climatology is to refer to metadata as information about the measurement process, station circumstances, and data. The term "data" is reserved solely for the actual weather and climate records obtained from sensors.

1.4.3. Maintenance

Inattention to maintenance is the greatest source of failure in weather/climate stations and networks. Problems begin to occur as soon as sites are deployed. A regular visit schedule must be implemented, where sites, settings (e.g., vegetation), sensors, communications, and data flow are checked routinely (once or twice a year at a minimum) and updated as necessary. Parts must be changed out for periodic recalibration or replacement. With adequate maintenance, the entire instrument suite should be replaced or completely refurbished about once every five to seven years.

Simple preventative maintenance is effective but requires much planning and skilled technical staff. Changes in technology and products require retraining and continual re-education. Travel, logistics, scheduling, and seasonal access restrictions can consume major amounts of time and budget but are absolutely necessary. Without such attention, data gradually become less credible and then often are misused or not used at all.

1.4.4. Automated versus Manual Stations

Historic stations often have depended on manual observations and many continue to operate in this mode. Manual observations frequently produce excellent data sets. Sensors and data are simple and intuitive, well tested, and relatively cheap. Manual stations have much to offer in certain circumstances and can be a source of both primary and backup data. However, methodical consistency for manual measurements is a constant challenge, especially with a mobile work force. Operating manual stations takes time and needs to be done on a regular schedule, though sometimes the routine is welcome.

Nearly all newer stations are automated. Automated stations provide better time resolution, increased (though imperfect) reliability, greater capacity for data storage, and improved accessibility to large amounts of data. The purchase cost for automated stations is higher than for manual stations. A common expectation and serious misconception is that an automated station can be deployed and left to operate on its own. In reality, automation does not eliminate the need for people but rather changes the type of person that is needed. Skilled technical personnel are needed and must be readily available, especially if live communications exist and data gaps are not wanted. Site visits are needed at least annually and spare parts must be maintained. Typical annual costs for sensors and maintenance are $1500–2500 per station.

1.4.5. Communications

With manual stations, the observer is responsible for recording and transmitting station data. Data from automated stations, however, can be transmitted quickly for access by research and operations personnel, which is a highly preferable situation. A comparison of communication systems for automated and manual stations shows that automated stations generally require additional equipment, more power, higher transmission costs, attention to sources of disruption or garbling, and backup procedures (e.g. manual downloads from data loggers).

Automated stations are capable of functioning normally without communication and retaining many months of data. At such sites, however, alerts about station problems are not possible, large gaps can accrue when accessible stations quit, and the constituencies needed to support such stations are smaller and less vocal. Two-way communications permit recovery in full from disruptions, ability to reprogram data loggers remotely, and better opportunities for diagnostics and troubleshooting. In virtually all cases, two-way communications are much preferred to all other communication methods. However, two-way communications require considerations of cost, signal access, transmission rates, interference, and methods for keeping sensor and communication power loops separate. Two-way communications are frequently impossible (no service) or impractical, expensive, or power consumptive. Two-way methods (cellular, land line, radio, Internet) require smaller up-front costs as compared to other methods of communication and have variable recurrent costs, starting at zero. Satellite links work everywhere (except when blocked by trees or cliffs) and are quite reliable but are one-way and relatively slow, allow no re-transmissions, and require high up-front costs ($3–4K) but no recurrent costs. Communications technology is changing constantly and requires vigilant attention by maintenance personnel.

1.4.6. Quality Assurance and Quality Control

Quality control and quality assurance are issues at every step through the entire sequence of sensing, communication, storage, retrieval, and display of environmental data. Quality assurance is an umbrella concept that covers all data collection and processing (start-to-finish) and ensures that credible information is available to the end user. Quality control has a more limited scope and is defined by the International Standards Organization as "the operational techniques and activities that are used to satisfy quality requirements." The central problem can be better appreciated if we approach quality control in the following way.

- Quality control is the evaluation, assessment, and rehabilitation of imperfect data by utilizing other imperfect data.

The quality of the data only decreases with time once the observation is made. The best and most effective quality control, therefore, consists in making high-quality measurements from the start and then successfully transmitting the measurements to an ingest process and storage site. Once the data are received from a monitoring station, a series of checks with increasing complexity can be applied, ranging from single-element checks (self-consistency) to multiple-element checks (inter-sensor consistency) to multiple-station/single-element checks (inter-station consistency). Suitable ancillary data (battery voltages, data ranges for all measurements, etc.) can prove extremely useful in diagnosing problems.

There is rarely a single technique in quality control procedures that will work satisfactorily for all situations. These procedures must be tailored to individual station circumstances, data access and storage methods, and climate regimes.

The fundamental issue in quality control centers on the tradeoff between falsely rejecting good data (Type I error) and falsely accepting bad data (Type II error). We cannot reduce the incidence of one type of error without increasing the incidence of the other type. In weather and climate data assessments, Type I errors are deemed far less desirable than Type II errors.

Not all observations are equal in importance. Quality-control procedures are likely to have the greatest difficulty evaluating the most extreme observations, where independent information usually must be sought and incorporated. Quality-control procedures involving more than one station usually involve a great deal of infrastructure with its own (imperfect) error-detection methods, which must be in place before a single value can be evaluated.

1.4.7. Standards

Although there is near-universal recognition of the value of systematic weather and climate measurements, these measurements will have little value unless they conform to accepted standards. There is not a single source for standards for collecting weather and climate data nor a single standard that meets all needs. Measurement standards have been developed by the American Association of State Climatologists (AASC 1985), U.S. Environmental Protection Agency (EPA 1987), World Meteorological Organization (WMO 1983; 2005), Finklin and Fischer (1990), National Wildfire Coordinating Group (2004), and RAWS program (Bureau of Land Management (BLM) 1997). Variations to these measurement standards also have been offered by instrument makers (e.g., Tanner 1990).

1.4.8. Who Makes the Measurements?

The lands under NPS stewardship provide many excellent locations to host the monitoring of climate by the NPS or other collaborators. Most park units historically have observed weather/climate elements as part of their overall mission. Many of these measurements come from station networks managed by other agencies, with observations taken or overseen by NPS personnel, in some cases, or by collaborators from the other agencies. National Park Service units that are small, lack sufficient resources, or lack sites presenting adequate exposure may benefit by utilizing weather/climate measurements collected from nearly stations.

2.0. Climate Background

Climate is one of the primary factors that determine how ecosystems evolve, differ from each other, and vary from one landscape to another (Jenny 1941). Impacts on natural systems due to global- and regional-scale climate variations are particularly pronounced in island systems (HaySmith et al. 2005), highlighting the importance of weather and climate monitoring efforts in these island systems. More detail is provided here on important factors shaping the climate zones and ecosystems in the islands.

Climate monitoring is also critical in order to properly manage the cultural resources of the PACN. Reverence for various aspects of weather and climate has been common among Pacific Islanders. These weather and climate features were often honored in song and dance. Much of this rich cultural heritage may be threatened by future regional- and global-scale climatic changes. For example, sea-level fluctuations may threaten low-lying cultural sites (HaySmith et al. 2005). It is therefore essential to understand the climate characteristics of the PACN. These characteristics are discussed in this chapter.

2.1. Climate and the PACN Environment

The dominant factor shaping the PACN climate is the tropical marine setting, characterized by relatively warm temperatures and minimal daily and seasonal temperature fluctuations. The vast Pacific Ocean dampens the temperature fluctuations and leads to a constant high relative humidity. Moderate wet and dry seasons exist throughout the region, yet these seasons are not synchronous among the various islands in the PACN (Figure 2.1). For example, in American Samoa (Figure 2.1a) the wet season lasts from October to May, in the Marianas from July to November (Figure 2.1b), in most of Hawaii from October to April (Figure 2.1c), and in some portions of Hawaii from April to September (Figure 2.1d).

a)

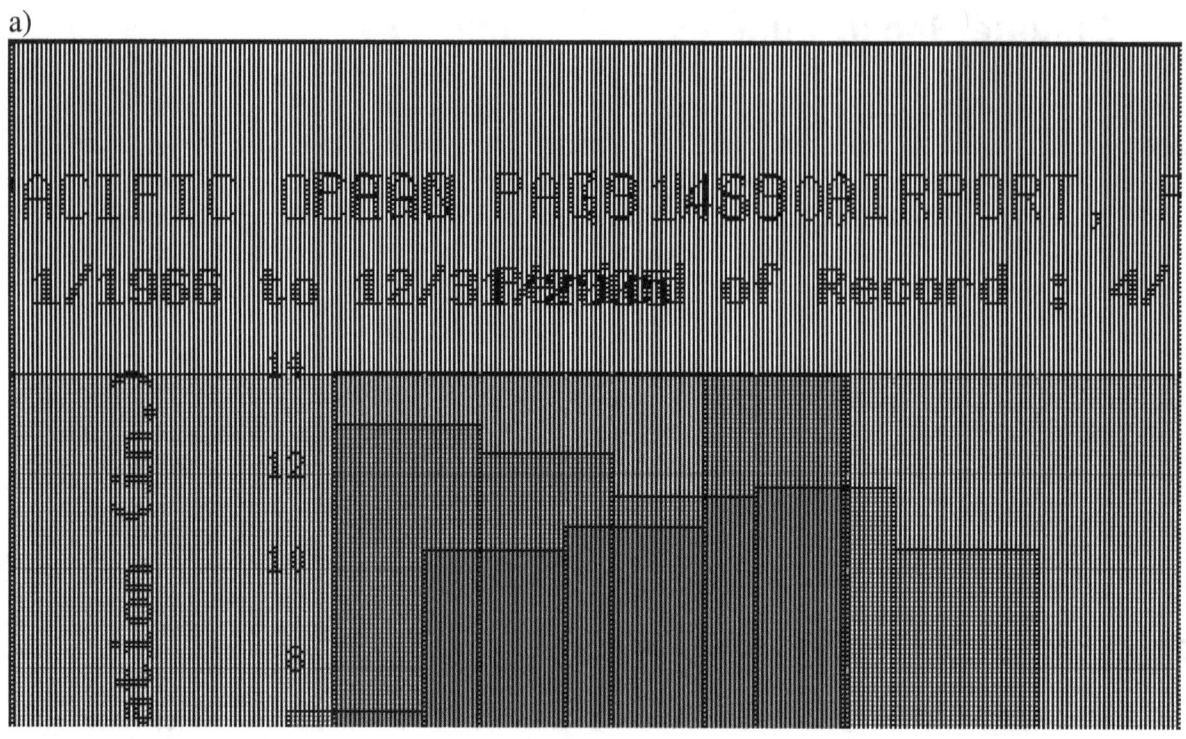

b)

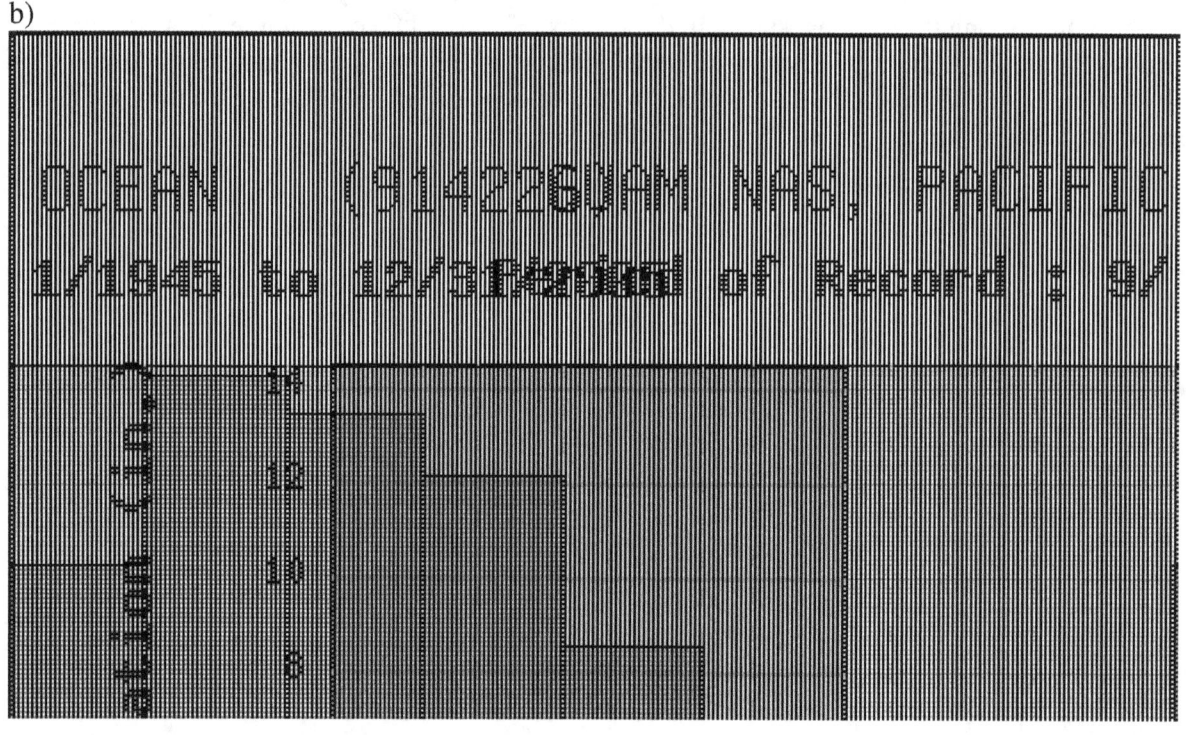

12

c)

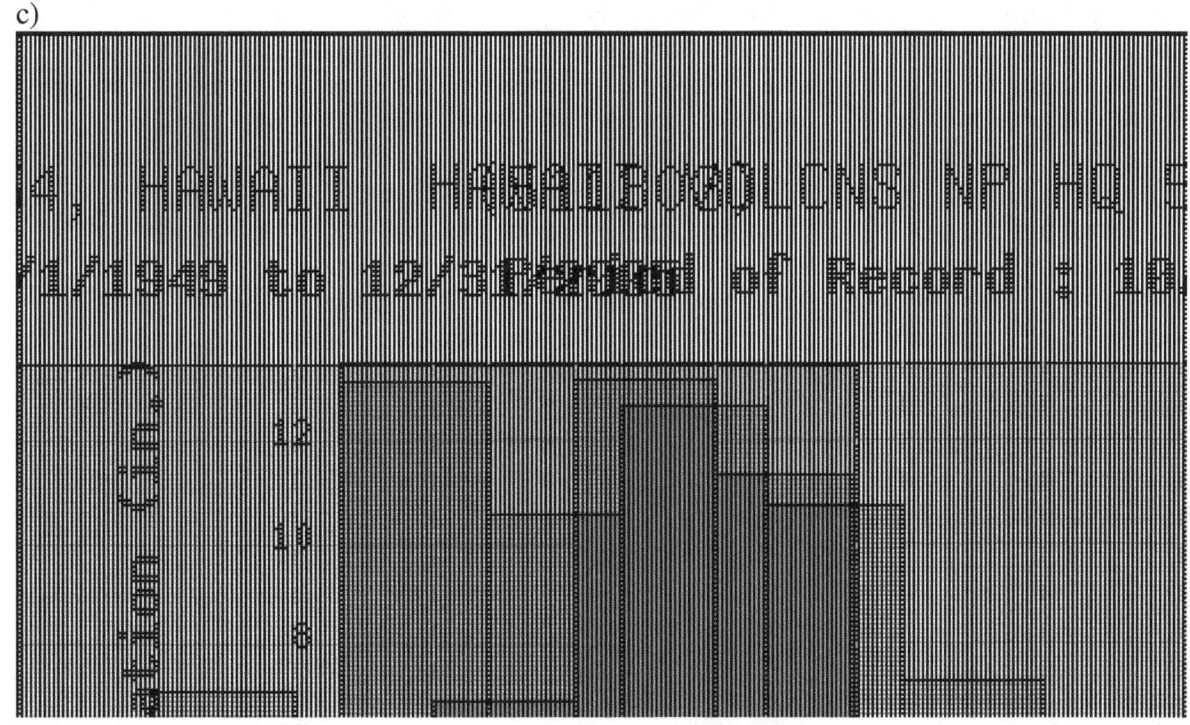

d)

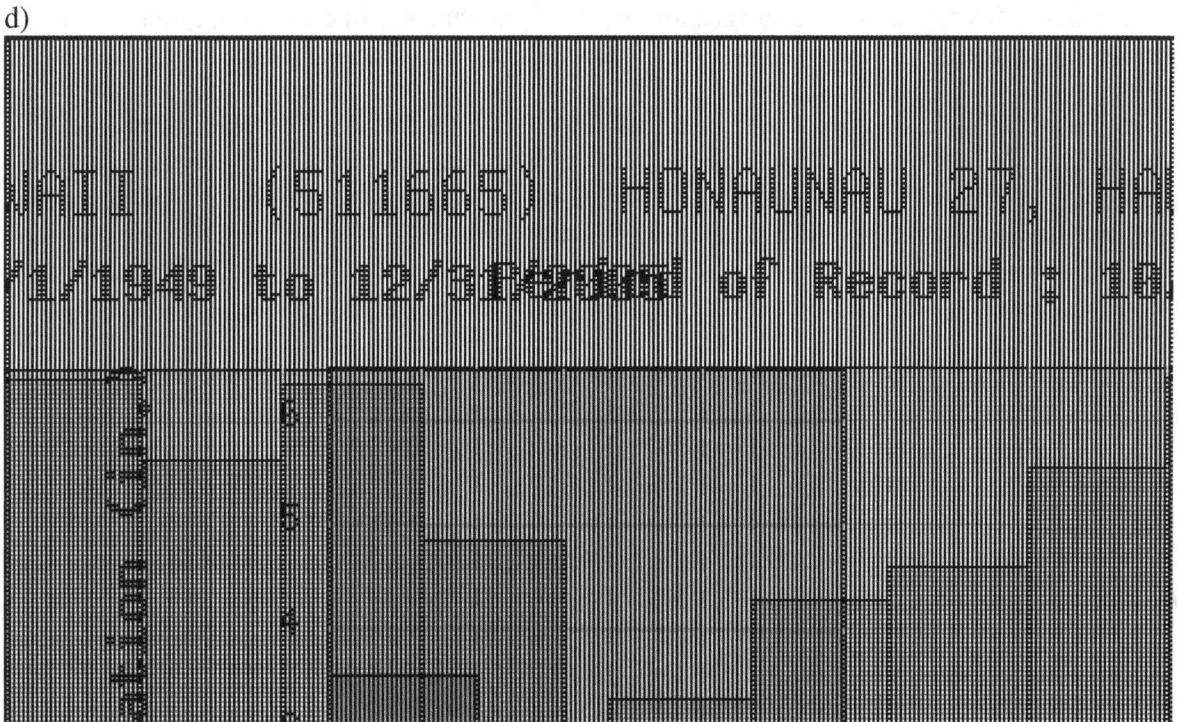

Figure 2.1. Mean monthly precipitation at American Samoa (a), Guam (b), and the Hawaiian Islands (c,d).

The PACN climate is strongly influenced by the Hadley cell, which describes the global circulation pattern in these latitudes (Trewartha and Horn 1980; Shea et al. 1991). Trade winds, or tropical easterlies, are common in PACN and develop along the equatorward side of the large anticyclones that dominate the subtropical oceans of the world. The PACN park units are generally poleward of the Intertropical Convergence Zone and are thus influenced by a feature called the trade wind inversion (see Appendix B). This feature develops in the following way. Middle and upper levels of the subtropical atmosphere are characterized by subsiding air in the Hadley cell. This subsiding air dries and warms as a result of compression. At the same time, moist air rising from the surface cools. At the meeting point of these two air masses, warm air overlays cool air, forming an inversion. The height of the trade wind inversion generally increases towards the west in the Pacific Ocean (Trewartha and Horn 1980). The presence of the trade wind inversion is an important factor influencing PACN ecology as it creates distinct zones along elevation gradients on the taller islands. Orographic uplift of moist air masses is capped by the warmer and much drier overlying air, forming a persistent cloud belt just below the inversion that supports cloud and rain forest habitat.

Climatic consequences of the El Niño-Southern Oscillation (ENSO) are much more pronounced in the PACN than on the North American continent and the rest of the world. Warm ENSO (El Niño) phases are characterized by unusually warm waters over the eastern and central equatorial Pacific; the opposite is true during cool ENSO (La Niña) phases. A complete ENSO cycle typically occurs once every 3-7 years. Climatic variations resulting from ENSO are dependent on sea surface temperature and thus vary throughout the PACN. These variations include changes to wind patterns, such as slowing or even reversal of the trade wind regime; increased tropical cyclone frequency; increased sea surface temperature; and changes in drought and flood frequency and intensity (Tsyban et al. 1990; Shea et al. 2001; Schlappa 2005).

Large-scale climate changes may also be partly responsible for the recent weakening of the Walker Circulation (see Appendix B), which is a large-scale zonal (east-west) overturning of air in the tropical Pacific Ocean (Vecchi et al. 2006) and is directly tied to the strength of the trade wind circulation and thus spatial precipitation patterns on the PACN islands. The strength of the Walker Circulation is believed to have decreased by just over three percent in the last century and may decrease by over ten percent according to climate change projections (Vecchi et al. 2006).

The above factors, along with significant variations in elevation within the PACN park units, act to create a wide diversity of climate zones on each of the islands of PACN (Giambelluca et al. 1986; HaySmith et al. 2005). This in turn sustains a great diversity of ecosystem types within the PACN parks. The land areas of the PACN are remotely located from continental land masses, and are also separated from each other by large distances. As a result of these isolative factors, the ecosystems of the PACN have developed a very unique and largely endemic set of native biota characteristics (Mittermeier et al. 1999). In addition, the PACN is also home to many of the threatened and endangered species of the U.S., providing some of the only remaining habitats for these species (Loope 1998; Olson et al. 2001; HaySmith et al. 2005).

The islands of the PACN are quite vulnerable to drought conditions, as the only freshwater resources are freshwater lenses and rainwater collection in tanks or reservoirs. An island's freshwater lens is created by groundwater recharge from rain; the size of a freshwater lens is directly proportional to the size of the island; thus, small islands are less buffered from drought conditions during which the lens is not recharged (Meehl 1996; Carter et al. 2001). Ground water use increases under drought conditions, leading to both rapid depletion of aquifers and salt water intrusion. Drought conditions also stress the flora and fauna of the PACN and lead to increased fire potential (Shea et al. 2001; Schlappa 2005).

Extreme events in the PACN, such as tropical cyclones, have severe, wide ranging and often long lasting effects on ecosystems (Herbert et al. 1999; Kennedy et al. 2002; Ostertag et al. 2003). Tropical cyclones generally hit American Samoa and the Hawaiian Islands once every few years, with greater frequency during El Niño periods. The island of Guam experiences the greatest number of tropical cyclones. These patterns are at least partially attributed to ocean temperatures around these islands. Tropical cyclones require ocean temperatures of at least 27°C or higher (Gray 1968). Ocean temperatures around the Hawaiian Islands are generally below this threshold, while ocean temperatures around Guam can easily exceed 30°C. If human-induced climate change leads to altered disturbance regimes, such as increased frequency and/or intensity of severe tropical cyclones, it will also lead to more severe damage and give ecosystems less time for recovery. There is no consensus among scientists on whether frequency of cyclones in the tropical Pacific will increase in the future (IPCC 2001). However, there seems to be agreement that future climate changes will lead to an increase in the intensity of storms (IPCC 2001; Shea et al. 2001).

Human-induced climate changes are expected to include much more rapid rates of change than have been experienced for millennia (Kennedy et al. 2002), leaving little time for natural systems to adapt. Island ecosystems, such as those in the PACN, are particularly vulnerable to the effects of climate change due to a combination of their geographic isolation and small size (Carter et al. 2001; Hay et al. 2001). Existing environmental stressors such as invasions by alien plant and animal species (Cuddihy and Stone 1990; Vitousek et al. 1996; Mueller-Dombois and Fosberg 1998; HaySmith et al. 2005) are driven by naturally- and anthropogenically-caused climatic changes. Land use changes such as forest clearing are likely to influence climate, especially at local and regional scales, through the alteration of surface energy budgets and rainfall patterns (Lawton et al. 2001). These changes will also influence ecosystem characteristics. Tropical forests in the PACN, for instance, are sensitive to changes in cloud cover and moisture (Stadtmueller 1987; Loope and Giambelluca 1998; Bruijnzeel 2000), both of which are affected by land use changes (Lawton et al. 2001).

Climate change will affect marine as well as terrestrial systems due to the impact of rising sea and air temperatures, sea level rise, increased erosion and runoff, changes to wind and precipitation patterns and possibly an increase in intensity and frequency of storms. Pacific islands are particularly vulnerable to sea level changes, which occur both as periodic variations associated with ENSO events and as longer-term trends. There is currently no consistent trend for sea level in the Pacific Basin; sea level has increased in some areas, which is attributed to global climate change, while sea level has decreased in other areas as a result of geologic processes (Shea et al. 2001). Despite current conditions, sea levels are expected to rise in response to projected climate changes, which will tend to reduce the available freshwater resources of the PACN (Shea et al. 2001; Carter et al. 2001), with correspondingly adverse impacts on PACN ecosystems. Increases in sea surface temperatures and atmospheric carbon dioxide levels have been linked to coral bleaching, a severe threat to many coral reef ecosystems in the PACN (Brown 1996; Shea et al. 2001; Carter et al. 2001) Climate changes such as increases in atmospheric carbon dioxide have been linked to increased ocean acidification (Orr et al. 2005) which is directly associated with weakened physical structures of coral reefs (Andersson et al. 2003).

Monitoring of climate parameters in national parks will provide data to evaluate whether ecosystem changes are correlated with climate change. These climate monitoring efforts will also help the NPS educate the public about the effects of climate change, thus influencing public discourse and action on this topic. Monitoring climate will yield information that can be used for management decisions regarding habitats or species that are at risk.

2.2. Hawaiian Islands

2.2.1. Spatial Variability

The climate characteristics of the Hawaiian Islands are largely determined by their topography (Sanderson 1993; Shea et al. 2001). Mean temperatures at the highest elevations are generally between 5-10°C, while mean temperatures for coastal areas are generally between 20-25°C. For much of any given year, the Hawaiian Islands are positioned on the equatorward side of a semi-permanent area of high pressure. This feature creates the region's persistent trade winds, which come from the north and east. The high pressure area, and its related trade winds, is strongest during the warm season ("kau") from April to September (Shea et al. 2001). These prevailing wind characteristics interact with topographical features and cause precipitation to be greatest on the northeast (windward) sides of the islands. Many higher elevations on the windward sides of the islands commonly receive over 5000 mm of precipitation annually, with the highest annual precipitation totals of over 10000 mm/year occurring at Mt. Waialeale on Kauai (Giambelluca et al. 1986; Sanderson 1993). Precipitation drops off sharply on the south and west (leeward) sides of the islands, where some locations on the west side of the island of Hawaii receive on average under 250 mm of precipitation each year. The Puukohola Heiau National Historic Site (PUHE), for example, is located in one of these precipitation minima (HaySmith et al. 2005; Schlappa 2005).

Dry conditions dominate at the highest elevations on the Hawaiian Islands, such as the Mauna Kea and Mauna Loa summits. At these locations, annual precipitation can average under 500 mm/year (Giambelluca et al. 1986). Much of this dryness is directly related to the fact that these summit locations are situated above the trade wind inversion (Shea et al. 2001; HaySmith et al. 2005). Orographic precipitation processes associated with the trade wind flow cause precipitation to increase with elevation at the lower and middle elevations of the islands. This low-level rising motion, however, cannot penetrate the larger-scale subsidence which dominates at higher elevations as a result of the subtropical high that resides near the islands.

The largest two Hawaiian parks, HAVO and HALE, include within their boundaries several climatic zones with a range of rainfall regimes. These rainfall regimes are largely defined by the interaction of the trade winds and the regional topography, where elevations range from sea level to just under 4200 m (14000 ft) at the summits of Mauna Kea and Mauna Loa. Two of the four rainfall minima on the island of Hawaii are found in HAVO. These two minima are located at the Kau Desert, which has a mean annual rainfall of under 750 mm, and the upper slopes of Mauna Loa, which receives under 500 mm of mean annual precipitation. Some of the precipitation on Mauna Loa falls as snow during the winter months. The highest mean annual rainfall within the park is found in Olaa Tract, a rain forest that receives over 4000 mm per year (Giambelluca et al. 1986). In general, the eastern windward portion of HAVO has high rainfall, which diminishes upslope, particularly above the trade wind inversion layer near 1800 m (6000 ft) elevation. In contrast, the leeward, western portions of HAVO are in rain shadows of Mauna Loa and Kilauea summit, and are typically dry. Like HAVO, HALE also has a range of climates, as it extends from sea level on the windward, eastern slope of Haleakala to the summit of East Maui. This park unit also includes lands in the leeward rain shadow of Haleakala, down to 1200 m (4000 ft) elevation. Annual precipitation in the park varies from 1250 mm in the crater, the southern slope, and Kaupo Gap to over 6000 mm on the northeastern slopes of Haleakala.

2.2.2. Temporal Variability

The warmer and drier months on the Hawaiian Islands are during the months of April to September (the "kau" season) while the cooler and wetter months are the "hooilo" season from October to March (Shea et al. 2001). This seasonal cycle is more pronounced on the leeward sides of the islands (Giambelluca et al. 1986). The region is heavily influenced by the ENSO cycle. Drought conditions are generally experienced on the islands every 3-7 years, in tandem with El Niño events.

Although the prevailing trade wind patterns provide generally homogenous climate conditions through time, this pattern can be disrupted in at least two key ways. For instance, "Kona storms" are upper-level low pressure centers of subtropical origin which form near the Hawaiian Islands during the winter months. The locations of these storms can vary from year to year. The most damaging Kona storms set up just to the west of the Hawaiian Islands, with their southerly flow of moisture bringing extended periods (often more than one week) of steady, persistent rainfall. During one such storm event in March, 2006, the visitor center at HAVO received over 700 mm of rain, almost one-third of the average annual rainfall at this location. The prevailing trade wind pattern can also be disrupted by tropical cyclones that can impact the region in El Niño years (Shea et al. 2001; Sanderson 1993).

2.3. Guam and Saipan

2.3.1. Spatial Variability

Guam, on which War In The Pacific National Historical Park (WAPA) is located, and the Northern Marianas have climates that are warm and tropical, with temperatures throughout the year averaging between 20-30°C (HaySmith et al. 2005). The average rainfall at sea level is just under 2200 mm on both the Northern Marianas (Baker 1951) and on Guam (Mueller-Dombois and Fosberg 1998). Although these islands are influenced by the same trade wind patterns as the Hawaiian Islands, the trade wind inversion is not as prominent as for the Hawaiian Islands

(Trewartha and Horn 1980) and their lack of significant topography does not induce a well-established rainshadow effect (HaySmith et al. 2005).

2.3.2. Temporal Variability

Guam and the Northern Marianas have consistently warm temperatures between 20°C and 35°C throughout the year (Schlappa 2005). They also have significant dry and rainy seasons, with transitional periods in between. The dry season is from January to April, while the wet season lasts from July to November (Shea et al. 2001). A few tropical cyclones influence this region each year but during El Niño years, the frequency of tropical cyclones increases, along with corresponding flooding events (Shea et al. 2001; HaySmith et al. 2005; Schlappa 2005).

2.4. American Samoa

2.4.1. Spatial Variability

Some of the islands of American Samoa do have significant topographic features with a well-established rainshadow effect much like the Hawaiian Islands. The highest elevations of these islands are over 800 m. The island of Tau receives more than 2500 mm per year, on average (Schlappa 2005). On the island of Tutuila, annual rainfall averages 3200 mm at the airport and some of the windward slopes receive over 5000 mm of rain every year (Shea et al. 2001; HaySmith et al. 2005; Schlappa 2005).

2.4.2. Temporal Variability

The islands of American Samoa have a warm tropical climate with little seasonal variation in temperature. Average air temperatures vary between 28°C in January and 26°C in July. The islands of American Samoa have pronounced dry and wet seasons. The dry season lasts from about June to September, while the wet season lasts from October through May (Shea et al. 2001; HaySmith et al. 2005). Occasional periods of significant drought do affect the islands (Whistler 1992). The ENSO cycle plays a key role in the region's interannual climatic variability. Tropical cyclones are not a regular occurrence, but during El Niño years, the frequency of tropical cyclones increases, along with corresponding flooding events (Whistler 1994).

3.0. Methods

Having discussed the climatic characteristics of the PACN, we now present the procedures that were used to obtain information for weather/climate stations within the PACN. This information was obtained from various sources, as mentioned in the following paragraphs. Retrieval of station metadata constituted a major component of this work.

3.1. Metadata Retrieval

A key component of station inventories is determining the kinds of observations that have been conducted over time, by whom, and in what manner; when each type of observation began and ended; and whether these observations are still being conducted. Metadata about the observational process generally consist of a series of vignettes that apply to time intervals and, therefore, constitute a *history* rather than a single snapshot. This report has relied on metadata records from three sources: (a) Western Regional Climate Center (WRCC), (b) NPS personnel, and (c) other knowledgeable personnel, such as state climate office staff. Metadata (Table 3.1) have been obtained as completely as possible for weather/climate stations in and near the park units within PACN. An expanded list of relevant metadata fields for this inventory is provided in Appendix D.

Table 3.1. Primary metadata fields with explanations, as appropriate, for the inventory of weather/ climate stations within the PACN.

Metadata Field	Notes
Station name	Station name associated with network listed in "Climate Network."
Latitude	Numerical value (units: see coordinate units).
Longitude	Numerical value (units: see coordinate units).
Coordinate units	Latitude/longitude (units: decimal degrees, degree-minute-second, etc.).
Datum	Datum used as basis for coordinates: WGS 84, NAD 83, etc.
Elevation	Elevation of station above mean sea level (m).
Slope	Slope of ground surface below station (degrees).
Aspect	Azimuth that ground surface below station faces.
Climate division	NOAA climate division where station is located. Climate divisions are NOAA-specified zones sharing similar climate and hydrology characteristics.
Country	Country where station is located.
State	State where station is located.
County	County where station is located.
Climate network	Weather/climate network where station resides.
NPS unit code	Four-letter code identifying park unit where station resides.
NPS unit name	Full name of park unit.
NPS unit type	National park, national monument, etc.
UTM zone	If UTM is the only coordinate system available.
Location notes	Useful information not already included in "station narrative."
Climate variables	Temperature, precipitation, etc.
Station type	Primary network the station belongs to (RAWS, COOP, etc.)

Metadata Field	Notes
Installation date	Date of station installation.
Removal date	Date of station removal.
Station photograph	Digital image of station.
Photograph date	Date photograph was taken.
Photographer	Name of person who took the photograph.
Station narrative	Anything related to general site description; may include site exposure, characteristics of surrounding vegetation, driving directions, etc.
Contact name	Name of the person involved with station operation.
Organization	Group or agency affiliation of contact person.
Contact type	Designation that identifies contact person as the station owner, observer, maintenance person, data manager, etc.
Position/job title	Official position/job title of contact person.
Address	Address of contact person.
E-mail address	E-mail address of contact person.
Phone	Phone number of contact person (and extension if available).
Contact notes	Other information needed to reach contact person.

The initial metadata sources for this report were stored at WRCC. This regional climate center (RCC) acts as a working repository of many western climate records, including the main networks outlined in this section. Live and periodic ingests from all major national and western weather/climate networks are maintained at WRCC. These networks include the COOP network; the Surface Airways Observation Network (SAO) jointly operated by NOAA and the Federal Aviation Administration (FAA); the NOAA upper-air observation network; NOAA data buoys; the interagency RAWS system; and various smaller networks. The WRCC is expanding its capability to ingest information from other networks as resources permit and usefulness dictates. This center has relied heavily on historic archives (in many cases supplemented with live ingests) to assess the quantity (not necessarily quality) of data available for NPS I&M network applications.

This report has relied primarily on metadata stored in the Applied Climate Information System (ACIS), a joint effort among RCCs and other NOAA entities. Metadata for PACN weather/climate stations identified from the ACIS database are available in file "PACN_from_ACIS.tar.gz" (see Appendix G). Historic metadata pertaining to major climate- and weather-observing systems in the United States are stored in ACIS where metadata are linked to the observed data. A distributed system, ACIS is synchronized among the RCCs. Mainstream software is utilized, including Postgress, Python™, and Java™ programming languages; CORBA®-compliant network software; and industry-standard, nonproprietary hardware and software. Metadata and data for all major national climate and weather networks have been entered into the ACIS database. For this project, the available metadata from many smaller networks also have been entered but in most cases the actual data have not yet been entered. Data sets are in the NetCDF (Network Common Data Form) format, but the design allows for integration with legacy systems, including non-NetCDF files (used at WRCC) and additional metadata (added for this project). The ACIS also supports a suite of products to visualize or summarize data from these data sets. National climate-monitoring maps are updated daily using the ACIS data feed. The developmental phases of ACIS have utilized metadata supplied by the NCDC and NWS with many tens of thousands of entries, screened as well as possible for duplications, mistakes, and omissions.

In addition to obtaining PACN weather/climate station metadata from ACIS, metadata were also obtained from NPS staff at the PACN office at HAVO. The metadata provided from the PACN office are available in the attached file "PACN_NPS.tar.gz" (Appendix G). Note that there is some overlap between the metadata provided from PACN and the metadata obtained from ACIS. We have also relied on information supplied at various times in the past by BLM, NPS, NCDC, NWS, the Hawaii Department of Land and Natural Resources, and the Hawaii state climate office (Table 3.2).

Table 3.2. Additional sources of weather and climate metadata for the PACN.

Name	Position	Phone Number	Email Address
Neal Fujii	State Drought Coordinator	(808)587-0264	neal.d.fujii@hawaii.gov
Pao-Shin Chu	Hawaii State Climatologist	(808)956-2324	chu@soest.hawaii.edu

Two types of information have been used to complete the climate station inventory for the PACN.

- Station inventories: Information about operational procedures, latitude/longitude, elevation, measured elements, measurement frequency, sensor types, exposures, ground cover and vegetation, data-processing details, network, purpose, and managing individual or agency, etc.

- Data inventories: Information about measured data values including start and end dates, completeness, properties of data gaps, representation of missing data, flagging systems, how special circumstances are denoted in the data record, etc.

This is not a straightforward process. Extensive searches are typically required to develop historic station and data inventories. Both types of inventories frequently contain information gaps and often rely on tacit and unrealistic assumptions. Sources of information for these inventories frequently are difficult to recover or are undocumented and unreliable. In many cases, the actual weather/climate data available from different sources are not linked directly to metadata records. To the extent that actual data can be acquired (rather than just metadata), it is possible to cross-check these records and perform additional assessments based on the amount and completeness of the data.

Certain types of weather/climate networks that possess any of the following attributes have not been considered for inclusion in the inventory:

- Private networks with proprietary access and/or inability to obtain or provide sufficient metadata.

- Private weather enthusiasts (often with high-quality data) whose metadata are not available and whose data are not readily accessible.
- Unofficial observers supplying data to the NWS (lack of access to current data and historic archives; lack of metadata).
- Networks having no available historic data.
- Networks having poor-quality metadata.
- Networks having poor access to metadata.
- Real-time networks having poor access to real-time data.

Previous inventory efforts at WRCC have shown that for the weather networks identified in the preceding list, in light of the need for quality data to track weather and climate, the resources required (often very substantial) and difficulty encountered in obtaining metadata or data are prohibitively large.

3.2. Criteria for Locating Stations

We included all weather and climate stations located on any of the islands in PACN. Due to the small size of the islands in PACN, we deemed it to be important to include all available stations for this inventory.

The station locator maps presented in Chapter 4 were designed to show clearly the spatial distributions of all major weather/climate station networks in PACN. We recognize that other mapping formats may be more suitable for other specific needs.

4.0. Station Inventory

An objective of this report is to show the locations of weather/climate stations for the PACN region in relation to the boundaries of the NPS park units within the PACN. A station does not have to be within park boundaries to provide useful data and information for a park unit.

4.1. Climate/Weather Networks

Most stations we have identified in the PACN are associated with at least one of nine major weather/climate networks (Table 4.1). Brief descriptions of each weather/climate network are provided in the following table (see Appendix F for greater detail).

Table 4.1. Weather/Climate networks represented within the PACN.

Acronym	Name
CASTNet	Clean Air Status and Trends Network
COOP	NWS Cooperative Observer Program
CRN	NOAA Climate Reference Network
CWOP	Citizen Weather Observer Program
GPMP	Gaseous Pollutant Monitoring Program
GPSMET	The University Center for Atmospheric Research GPS/MET Experiment
OBOP	NOAA Earth Systems Research Laboratory Observatory Operations Group
RAWS	Remote Automated Weather Station
SAO	NWS/FAA Surface Airways Observation Network

4.1.1. Clean Air Status and Trends Network (CASTNet)

CASTNet is primarily an air-quality monitoring network managed by the EPA. Standard hourly meteorologic elements are measured and include temperature, wind, humidity, solar radiation, soil temperature, and sometimes soil moisture. These elements are intended to support interpretation of air-quality parameters that also are measured at CASTNet sites. Data records at CASTNet sites are generally one–two decades in length.

4.1.2. NWS Cooperative Observer Program (COOP)

The COOP network has been a foundation of the U.S. climate program for decades. Manual measurements are made by volunteers and consist of daily maximum and minimum temperatures, observation-time temperature, and daily precipitation. Many of the COOP sites in PACN are precipitation-only sites. The quality of data from COOP sites ranges from excellent to modest.

4.1.3. NOAA Climate Reference Network (CRN)

The CRN is intended as a reference network for the U.S. that meets the requirements of the Global Climate Observing System. Up to 115 CRN sites are planned for installation, but the actual number of installed sites will depend on available funding. Temperature and precipitation are the primary meteorological elements are measured. Wind, solar radiation, and ground surface temperature are also measured. Data from the CRN are intended for use in operational climate-monitoring activities and to place current climate patterns in historic perspective.

4.1.4. Citizen Weather Observer Program (CWOP)

The CWOP network consists primarily of automated weather stations operated by private citizens who have either an Internet connection and/or a wireless Ham radio setup. Data from CWOP stations are specifically intended for use in research, education, and homeland security activities. Although meteorological elements such as temperature, precipitation, and wind are measured at all CWOP stations, station characteristics do vary, including sensor types and site exposure.

4.1.5. NPS Gaseous Pollutant Monitoring Program (GPMP)

The GPMP network measures hourly meteorological data in support of pollutant monitoring activities. Measured elements include temperature, precipitation, humidity, wind, solar radiation, and surface wetness. These data are generally of high quality, with records extending up to 1-2 decades in length.

4.1.6. The GPS/MET Experiment (GPSMET)

The GPS/MET Experiment is conducted through the University Center for Atmospheric Research. The objective of GPSMET stations is to use signals from GPS satellites to demonstrate active atmospheric limb sounding. Temperature, pressure, and humidity are measured at atmospheric levels extending from the surface to the ionosphere.

4.1.7. NOAA Earth Systems Research Laboratory Observatory Operations Group (OBOP)

The NOAA Earth Systems Research Laboratory operates five atmospheric baseline observatories worldwide. These stations monitoring atmospheric concentrations of carbon dioxide and other trace gases, with meteorological measurements being conducted in support of this mission. These stations started taking observations in the 1950s or later. These stations measure temperature, precipitation, wind speed and direction, wind gusts, pressure, and solar radiation.

4.1.8. Remote Automated Weather Station Network (RAWS)

The RAWS network is administered through many natural resource management agencies, particularly the BLM and the Forest Service. Hourly meteorology elements are measured and include temperature, wind, humidity, solar radiation, barometric pressure, fuel temperature, and precipitation (when temperatures are above freezing). The fire community is the primary client for RAWS data. These sites are remote and data typically are transmitted via GOES (Geostationary Operational Environmental Satellite). Some sites operate all winter. Most data records for RAWS sites began during or after the mid-1980s.

4.1.9. NWS/FAA Surface Airways Observation Network (SAO)

These stations are located usually at major airports and military bases. These include Automated Surface Observing System (ASOS) and Automated Weather Observing System (AWOS) sites. Almost all SAO sites are automated. The hourly data measured at these sites include temperature, precipitation, humidity, wind, pressure, sky cover, ceiling, visibility, and current weather. Most data records begin during or after the 1940s, and these data are generally of excellent quality.

4.1.10. Other Networks

We are aware of weather and climate stations that are associated with HaleNet (Haleakala Climate Network). This network consists of two climate station transects on the slopes of Haleakala Volcano in HALE. One transect is on the windward side of the volcano, while the other transect is on the leeward side. This network has been operated in support of various research efforts within HALE, including the monitoring of invasive plant and animal species. We are also aware of several weather stations that are part of the Mauna Kea Weather Center, on the summit of Mauna Kea. Finally, we are aware of U.S. Geological Survey (USGS) precipitation stations that are in or near PACN park units, along with manual stations that have been identified with the National Fire Danger Rating System (NFDRS) program. It is anticipated that the stations identified from these networks (see Appendix H) will be added to the final versions of the metadatabase files accompanying this report.

In addition to the major networks mentioned above, there are various networks that are operated for specific purposes by specific organizations or governmental agencies or scientific research projects. These networks could be present within PACN but have not been identified in this report. Some of the commonly used networks include the following:

- USGS- and university-administered volcano monitoring networks
- NOAA upper-air stations
- National Atmospheric Deposition Program (NADP)
- Federal and state departments of transportation
- National Science Foundation Long-Term Ecological Research Network
- U.S. Department of Energy Surface Radiation Budget Network (Surfrad)
- Various U.S. Military sites monitoring nuclear releases with all weapons storage
- Other research or project networks having many possible owners

4.2. Station Locations

The major weather/climate networks in PACN (discussed in Section 4.1) have up to a few stations in each park unit (Table 4.2). Most of these stations are COOP or RAWS stations. The greatest numbers of weather/climate stations are located in HALE and HAVO. The Ala Kahakai National Historic Trail (ALKA) connects PUHE, KAHO, PUHO and HAVO. Therefore, any station located in one of the Hawaii Island parks is also relevant to ALKA. Once GPS coordinates for the exact trail corridor have been determined it is likely that that more stations will be identified for this national historic trail as a considerable number of COOP stations are located near the coast.

Table 4.2. Number of stations inside PACN park units (listed by park unit and weather/climate network).

Weather/Climate Network	AMME	HALE	HAVO	KAHO	KALA
CASTNet	0	0	0	0	0
COOP	0	3	5	1	1
CRN	0	0	0	0	0
CWOP	0	0	0	0	0
GPMP	0	0	2	0	0
GPSMET	0	0	0	0	0
OBOP	0	0	1	0	0
RAWS	0	1	5	1	3
SAO	0	0	0	0	0
Network	**NPSA**	**PUHE**	**PUHO**	**USAR**	**WAPA**
CASTNet	0	0	0	0	0
COOP	1	1	0	0	1
CRN	0	0	0	0	0
CWOP	0	0	0	0	0
GPMP	0	0	0	0	0
GPSMET	0	0	0	0	0
OBOP	0	0	0	0	0
RAWS	0	0	0	0	0
SAO	0	0	0	0	0

Lists of stations have been compiled for the PACN. A station does not have to be within the boundaries to provide useful data and information regarding the park unit in question. Some might be physically *within* the administrative or political boundaries, whereas others might be just outside, or even some distance away, but would be *nearby* in behavior and representativeness. What constitutes "useful" and "representative" are questions whose answers vary according to application, type of element, period of record, procedural or methodological observation conventions, and the like.

4.2.1. Hawaii

The Hawaiian Islands have extensive coverage of weather/climate stations on each of the islands containing PACN park units (Figure 4.1). It is worth noting that the Hawaiian Islands have a dense network of precipitation gauges. Although most of these are privately owned, these gauges are still useful for investigating spatial and temporal precipitation patterns over the islands (e.g. Giambelluca et al. 1986; Chu and Nakashima 2004).

The greatest concentrations of stations are found on the islands of Oahu and Maui. Most of these stations are situated closer to the coasts, while stations are less numerous inland, especially on the island of Hawaii. The COOP network has the greatest number of stations on these islands. The majority of COOP sites on the Hawaiian Islands measure only precipitation and have traditionally been associated with plantations in the area.

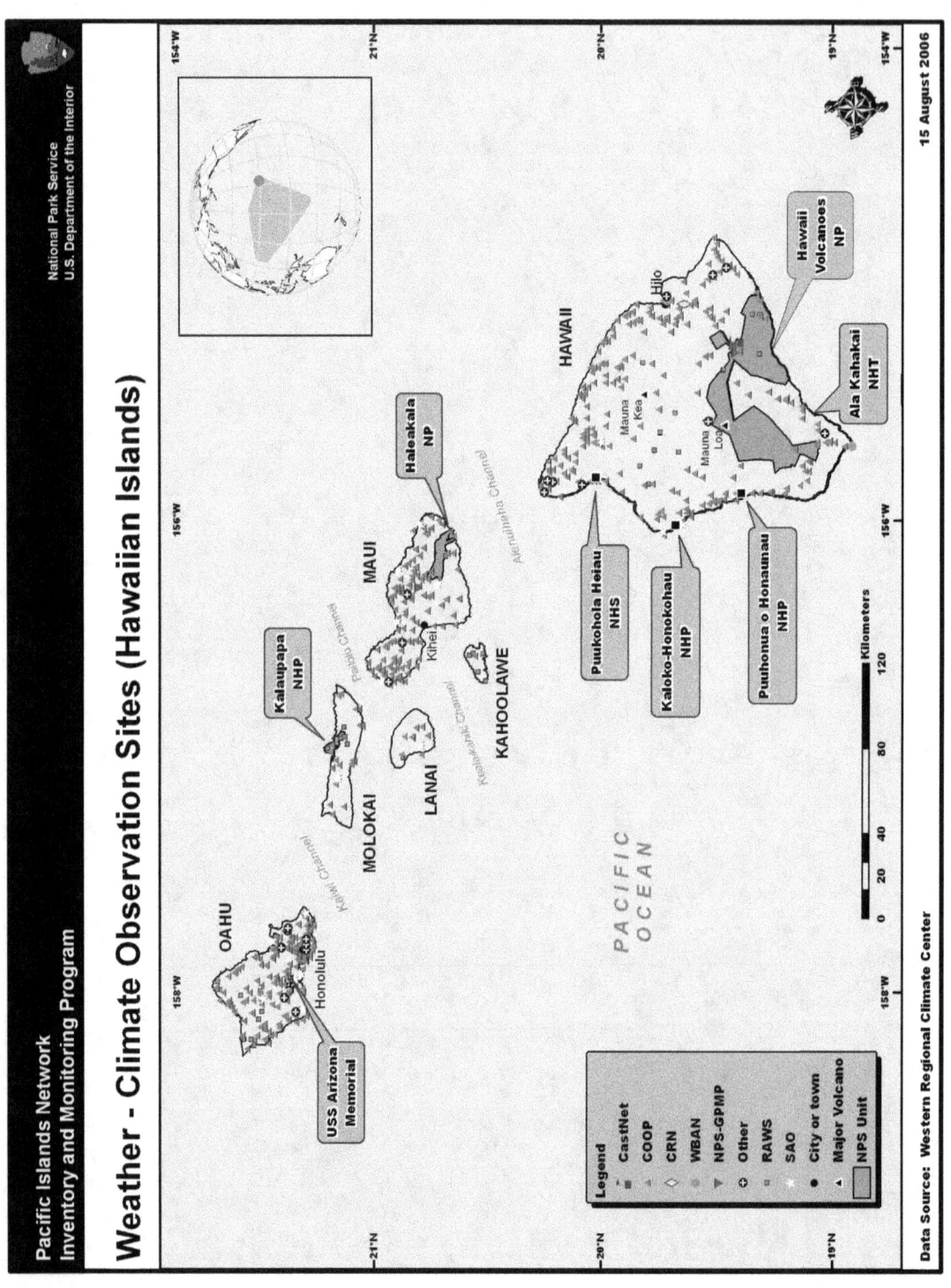

Figure 4.1. Station locations for the Hawaiian Islands park units.

The two largest park units on the Hawaiian Islands are HALE, on the island of Maui, and HAVO, on the island of Hawaii. Manual and automated stations are currently operating within both park units.

There are two currently-operating weather/climate stations within HALE (Table 4.3). One is a RAWS site at Kaupo Gap, which has been in operation since 1991. The other is a COOP site (Ohe'o 258.6) which has operated since 1982. This COOP site has measured precipitation since 1982 but has measured air temperature only since the late 1990s.

Just outside of HALE, a reliable long-term station is situated at Haleakala Summit. This site is associated with both the COOP and SAO networks and has made reliable weather observations since 1957 (Table 4.3). In addition to the SAO at Haleakala Summit, there are at least two other reliable SAO sites within 20 km of HALE. These are "Kailua 446", which has a data record extending back to 1947, and "Hana Airport 355", where data records extend back to 1950. Both of these SAO sites are co-located with COOP sites. Several COOP sites in the area have data records that approach 100 years in length (Table 4.3).

At least seven weather/climate stations are currently operating in HAVO (Table 4.3). Five of these are automated stations with near-real-time observations, while the other two are manual COOP stations. There are two GPMP stations, "Hawaii Volcanoes VC" and "Hawaii Volcanoes", which are currently in operation in HAVO. These sites have operated since 1986 and 1999, respectively. Two RAWS stations are currently taking observations in HAVO. Both of these stations started observations in 1999 and have high-quality data records.

The two COOP stations that are currently operating in HAVO are "Kealakomo 38.8" and "Halemaumau 52". The COOP site at "Kealakomo 38.8" is close to sea level and has only operated since 1995. The COOP site at "Halemaumau 52", situated at an elevation of just over 1100 m, measures only precipitation and has a data record extending back to 1949. Daily precipitation measurements were made at "Halemaumau 52" up until the early 1980s. After this time, precipitation has been measured only once weekly.

Besides the Mauna Loa Observatory, which is an OBOP station that is near the summit of Mauna Loa and has operated since 1955, there being no long-term records inside HAVO of other climate elements besides precipitation. However, the COOP site "Hawaii Volcanoes NP Hq. 54", near the east entrance of HAVO, has lengthy data records of both temperature and precipitation. These records extend from 1949 to present (Table 4.3), with generally high-quality data. Several COOP stations around HAVO have data records approaching 100 years in length (Table 4.3).

Additional automated weather observations are also available near HAVO. Reliable weather observations are being taken at a CRN station on the slopes of Mauna Loa just north of HAVO (Mauna Loa 5 NNE). This CRN site is at an elevation of about 3400 m and has operated for the last few years, complementing the data from Mauna Loa Observatory. Additional high-altitude measurements are provided at the Mauna Kea Weather Center, on Mauna Kea's summit. Another CRN station (Hilo 5 S) is operating about 30 km north and east of HAVO. A CASTNet site at Thurston Lava Tubes (elevation – 1199 m) provided automated weather observations from 1999-2004 but is not currently operating. However, measurements are still being taken at the

GPSMET site (Mauna Loa) that is co-located with the aforementioned CASTNet site. The nearest SAO site to HAVO is at Hilo International Airport, which is at sea level about 40 km north and east of HAVO. Data records at this station are generally of excellent quality and extend back to 1949 (Table 4.3).

Besides HALE and HAVO, the largest park unit on the Hawaiian Islands is KALA, on the island of Molokai. One RAWS site (Makapulapai) and two COOP sites (Kalaupapa 563, Waikolu 540) are currently in operation inside the boundaries of KALA. All three of these sites are located on the windward side of the island of Molokai. The RAWS station at Makapulapai has a data record extending back to 1993 (Table 4.3). The COOP site "Kalaupapa 563" measures both temperature and precipitation and has a data record extending back to 1933 (Table 4.3). Temperature observations are only available during the 1950s and from the late 1990s to present. Precipitation records for "Kalaupapa 563" are much more complete; however, there is a data gap during the 1960s. This COOP site has periodic observation gaps during weekends, especially during the last 2 decades. The COOP site "Waikolu 540" measures precipitation only and has a largely complete data record, with only occasional data gaps, extending back to 1965 (Table 4.3).

There is one SAO site (Molokai Kaunakakai Molokai Airport) located near the boundaries of KALA. This site is co-located with a COOP station and has a reliable, high-quality data record going back to 1940.

Two sites are currently operating at KAHO, one manual and one automated. The manual station is a COOP station (Honokohau Harbor 68.14), which has operated since 1991 (Table 4.3), while the automated station is a RAWS station (Kaloko-Honokohau), which has operated since 2004. The COOP station measures precipitation only but has a complete data record that is of high quality.

Outside KAHO, there are two nearby SAO stations currently in operation. The longest period of record is provided by the SAO station at Kona, going back to 1947 (Table 4.3). The data record for the other SAO station (Kailua Kona Ke-Ahole Ap.) extends back to 1970. Other than these two SAO sites, none of the stations listed for KAHO in Table 4.3 have reliable, long-term data records.

There is one COOP station that is currently operating at PUHE (Puukohola Heiau 98.1). This site measures both temperature and precipitation, and has a largely-complete data record that starts in 1976. There are no automated stations at PUHE. Automated stations and stations with longer data records are present outside PUHE, with the most reliable data coming from Waimea Kohala Airport. This location operates both a COOP station and a SAO station. The data records at this location extend back to 1953 (Table 4.3) and the data are of high quality. Other nearby stations have longer data records of both temperature and precipitation extending back to 1905 (e.g. Kawi 168 (COOP), Kohala Mission 175.1 (COOP)). However, these sites have frequent large gaps in both temperature and precipitation observations during the period of record.

There are no weather/climate stations currently in operation at PUHO. In fact, there are no automated stations listed in the vicinity of PUHO (Table 4.3). All of the stations are manual stations associated with the COOP network. The nearest COOP station is "Puuhonua-O-Hona

27.4", which has data starting from 1970 (Table 4.3). Although this site measures precipitation only, there are very few gaps in the data record. The COOP stations with the longest data records listed for PUHO include "Kealakekua 26.2", "Kainaliu 73.2", "Napoopoo 28", and "Honaunau 27" (precipitation only). Of these stations, "Kainaliu 73.2" provides the most complete data record of both temperature and precipitation. Data are available for "Kainaliu 73.2" from 1949 until the early 1980s, after which observations have generally not been taken on weekends.

Many of the weather and climate stations for KAHO, PUHE, and PUHO are also useful for climate monitoring efforts associated with ALKA, particularly the COOP stations. The only real-time weather observations along ALKA are provided by the SAO sites around KAHO (see Table 4.3).

The USS Arizona Memorial (USAR) currently has no on-site weather/climate stations. However, there are many nearby manual and automated stations providing weather and climate data for the greater Honolulu metropolitan area. Of the large number of stations near USAR, the closest automated and manual observations are provided from Honolulu International Airport (Table 4.3). This location operates both a COOP and a SAO station. Both stations have high-quality data records that extend back to 1946.

Table 4.3. Weather/climate stations for the Hawaiian Islands park units. Each listing includes station name, location, and elevation; weather/climate network associated with station; operational start/end dates for station; and flag to indicate if station is located inside park unit boundaries. Missing entries are indicated by "M".

Name	Lat.	Lon.	Elev. (m)	Network	Start	End	In Park?
Ala Kahakai National Historic Trail (ALKA)							
See weather/climate station lists for KAHO, PUHE, and PUHO							
Haleakala National Park (HALE)							
Holua Cabin 259.5	20.750	-156.217	2113	COOP	5/1/1964	10/1/1999	YES
Ohe'o 258.6	20.665	-156.047	37	COOP	2/1/1982	Present	YES
Panileihulu 259.2	20.678	-156.140	1088	COOP	10/1/1964	12/1/2005	YES
Kaupo Gap	20.684	-156.152	1229	RAWS	1/1/1991	Present	YES
Auwahi 252	20.624	-156.331	628	COOP	9/1/1963	7/1/1998	NO
Camp 10 HCS 402	20.867	-156.400	110	COOP	10/1/1949	4/30/1963	NO
Camp K 3 HCS 313	20.817	-156.433	79	COOP	10/1/1949	4/30/1963	NO
East Honomanu 345	20.817	-156.200	976	COOP	6/1/1950	2/28/1961	NO
Eke	20.917	-156.583	1403	COOP	1/1/1919	12/31/1930	NO
Fahinahina Camp 465.	20.958	-156.659	220	COOP	2/24/2003	Present	NO
Field 28 Reservoir 474.2	20.970	-156.640	351	COOP	11/23/2005	Present	NO
Field 46 474	20.989	-156.628	320	COOP	1/1/1991	10/18/2005	NO
Haelaau 477	20.938	-156.619	909	COOP	10/1/1949	Present	NO
Haiku 488.7	20.932	-156.325	107	COOP	2/24/2003	Present	NO
Haleakala Exp. Farm 4	20.850	-156.300	640	COOP	10/1/1939	10/30/1992	NO
Haleakala R.S. 338	20.764	-156.250	2122	COOP	3/1/1939	Present	NO
Haleakala Ranch 432	20.837	-156.319	576	COOP	1/1/1905	Present	NO
Haleakala Summit 338	20.717	-156.267	3038	COOP	4/1/1957	Present	NO

Name	Lat.	Lon.	Elev. (m)	Network	Start	End	In Park?
Haleakali	20.717	-156.250	2975	COOP	1/1/1923	12/31/1932	NO
Halehaku 492.2	20.916	-156.286	210	COOP	11/1/1991	Present	NO
Haliimaile 423	20.871	-156.344	326	COOP	1/1/1964	Present	NO
Hamakuapoko 485	20.926	-156.343	98	COOP	1/1/1942	Present	NO
Hamoa 282	20.717	-156.000	34	COOP	2/1/1942	1/31/1950	NO
Hana 354	20.750	-155.983	37	COOP	5/1/1907	12/21/1983	NO
Hana Airport 355	20.797	-156.017	23	COOP	12/1/1950	Present	NO
Hana Display Station	20.750	-155.983	0	COOP	M	Present	NO
Hanahuli 281	20.700	-156.017	101	COOP	4/1/1947	5/31/1976	NO
Hane Mauka	20.750	-156.033	525	COOP	1/1/1942	12/31/1945	NO
Holua Cabin 259.5	20.750	-156.217	2113	COOP	5/1/1964	10/1/1999	NO
Honokohau 480	20.965	-156.591	265	COOP	10/1/1949	Present	NO
Honokohua 493	21.001	-156.660	67	COOP	9/1/1919	Present	NO
Honokowai Intake 476	20.933	-156.617	476	COOP	1/1/1942	4/30/1963	NO
Honolua Field 49 494	21.014	-156.638	40	COOP	7/1/1907	8/1/2003	NO
Honomaele Mauka	20.767	-156.050	763	COOP	1/1/1942	12/31/1945	NO
Honomanu 450	20.850	-156.183	390	COOP	1/1/1905	2/28/1961	NO
Honomanu Gulch 341	20.778	-156.231	1915	COOP	1/1/1950	11/1/2000	NO
Honomanu Mauka 344	20.817	-156.200	894	COOP	10/1/1949	1/31/1950	NO
Horner Reservoir 467.01	20.926	-156.653	391	COOP	10/1/2001	5/1/2004	NO
Iao Needle 387.2	20.883	-156.550	329	COOP	2/1/1965	2/28/1978	NO
Kaanapali Airport 453.1	20.933	-156.700	2	COOP	10/1/1905	1/25/1986	NO
Kaeleku	20.783	-156.033	92	COOP	1/1/1927	12/31/1945	NO
Kahakuloa 482.4	20.957	-156.537	335	COOP	1/1/1923	Present	NO
Kahakuloa Mauka 482.	20.989	-156.548	198	COOP	12/1/1967	Present	NO
Kahoma Intake 374	20.905	-156.626	610	COOP	1/2/1919	Present	NO
Kahoolawe 499.6	20.557	-156.575	366	COOP	11/1/1989	Present	NO
Kahului Airport	20.900	-156.429	16	COOP	1/1/1905	Present	NO
Kahului Harbor	20.900	-156.467	0	COOP	9/1/1962	Present	NO
Kailiili 436	20.846	-156.274	768	COOP	3/13/1925	Present	NO
Kailua 446	20.893	-156.215	213	COOP	1/1/1905	Present	NO
Kailua Mauka 443	20.833	-156.233	966	COOP	10/1/1949	2/1/1961	NO
Kapalua W Maui Arpt. 462	20.966	-156.677	73	COOP	3/1/1987	Present	NO
Kauaula Intake 375	20.881	-156.626	485	COOP	1/1/1942	Present	NO
Kaupakulua	20.900	-156.300	320	COOP	1/1/1920	12/31/1938	NO
Kaupakulua 435.3	20.885	-156.286	427	COOP	12/1/1988	Present	NO
Kaupo Ranch 259	20.651	-156.139	311	COOP	2/1/1965	Present	NO
Keahua 410	20.864	-156.386	146	COOP	1/1/1942	Present	NO
Keanae 346	20.829	-156.168	299	COOP	1/1/1905	Present	NO
Keawakapu Beach 260.2	20.700	-156.450	6	COOP	4/1/1964	3/1/1982	NO
Kihei 311	20.794	-156.445	49	COOP	1/1/1905	Present	NO
Kihei No. 2 311.5	20.739	-156.447	43	COOP	2/24/2003	Present	NO
Kipahulu 258	20.650	-156.067	79	COOP	7/1/1916	4/30/1981	NO
Kole Kole	20.717	-156.267	3057	COOP	8/1/1952	8/31/1958	NO
Kuhiwa Camp 351	20.783	-156.117	946	COOP	10/1/1949	1/31/1950	NO
Kuiaha 490.7	20.893	-156.303	341	COOP	1/1/1993	7/29/2002	NO

Name	Lat.	Lon.	Elev. (m)	Network	Start	End	In Park?
Kula Branch Stn 324.5	20.762	-156.324	930	COOP	8/1/1978	Present	NO
Kula Erehwon 328	20.750	-156.317	1220	COOP	1/1/1905	12/31/1953	NO
Kula Heights 323.2	20.783	-156.317	769	COOP	1/1/1964	4/30/1977	NO
Kula Hospital 267	20.704	-156.359	916	COOP	7/1/1916	Present	NO
Lahaina 361	20.884	-156.681	12	COOP	7/1/1916	10/31/2001	NO
Lahaina WMDC	20.867	-156.683	0	COOP	M	Present	NO
Lahainaluna 361.1	20.892	-156.662	174	COOP	2/24/2003	Present	NO
Launiupoko Intk 376	20.858	-156.618	390	COOP	7/1/1916	Present	NO
Launiupoko Vllg 372	20.855	-156.649	67	COOP	1/1/1942	Present	NO
Lupi Upper 442	20.889	-156.248	378	COOP	1/1/1919	Present	NO
Maalaea Harbor	20.800	-156.517	0	COOP	12/1/1962	Present	NO
Mahana 473	20.967	-156.633	427	COOP	9/1/1919	11/30/1954	NO
Mahinahina 466	20.959	-156.651	299	COOP	9/1/1919	Present	NO
Makawao	20.850	-156.317	519	COOP	1/1/1905	12/31/1928	NO
Makena GC 249.1	20.645	-156.443	30	COOP	5/1/1982	Present	NO
Maluhia 482.2	20.950	-156.533	317	COOP	1/1/1966	12/31/1967	NO
Mokupea 475	20.983	-156.617	393	COOP	9/1/1919	6/1/1988	NO
Nakalalua 481	20.917	-156.600	1357	COOP	10/1/1949	3/31/1963	NO
Nakalele Field 60 49	21.028	-156.604	104	COOP	10/1/1949	Present	NO
Olinda #1 332	20.803	-156.277	1259	COOP	1/1/1919	Present	NO
Olowalu 296.1	20.816	-156.619	9	COOP	8/1/1916	Present	NO
Olowalu Gulch 377	20.850	-156.600	244	COOP	10/1/1949	2/29/1972	NO
Opana Mauka 440	20.833	-156.250	961	COOP	10/1/1949	2/28/1961	NO
Paakea 350	20.817	-156.122	384	COOP	1/1/1938	Present	NO
Paia 406	20.910	-156.377	52	COOP	1/1/1905	Present	NO
Pauwela 490	20.917	-156.317	149	COOP	1/1/1905	2/1/1970	NO
Peahi 488.6	20.900	-156.283	253	COOP	11/1/1976	9/30/1988	NO
Pohakea Bridge 307.2	20.819	-156.510	52	COOP	10/1/1949	Present	NO
Polipoli Springs 267	20.681	-156.333	1875	COOP	1/1/1964	Present	NO
Pukalani 426.6	20.839	-156.333	494	COOP	3/18/2003	Present	NO
Pulehu 315	20.833	-156.417	137	COOP	10/4/1949	4/30/1963	NO
Puohokamoa 2 343	20.826	-156.213	909	COOP	1/1/1919	Present	NO
Puu Kuku Upper No. 1	20.917	-156.583	1525	COOP	1/1/1919	12/31/1939	NO
Puu Kukui 380	20.895	-156.590	1765	COOP	10/1/1949	Present	NO
Puu Kukui Makai 472	20.917	-156.633	763	COOP	10/1/1949	2/29/1972	NO
Puu Kukui Upper No. 2	20.900	-156.600	1357	COOP	1/1/1923	12/31/1939	NO
Puu Paki 352	20.774	-156.057	659	COOP	12/1/1971	Present	NO
Puukolii 457	20.917	-156.683	110	COOP	10/1/1949	4/30/1963	NO
Puukolii 457.1	20.932	-156.676	128	COOP	6/1/1986	Present	NO
Puunene 396	20.875	-156.457	18	COOP	10/1/1949	Present	NO
Puunene CAA Airport	20.833	-156.467	40	COOP	10/1/1949	12/31/1958	NO
Puuomalei	20.867	-156.300	451	COOP	1/1/1910	12/31/1937	NO
Spreckelsville 400	20.897	-156.413	27	COOP	10/1/1949	Present	NO
Twin Gates 261.3	20.767	-156.383	399	COOP	1/1/1964	7/1/1986	NO
Ukulele 333	20.793	-156.249	1595	COOP	1/1/1905	Present	NO
Ukumehame 301	20.806	-156.585	24	COOP	1/1/1942	10/1/1999	NO

Name	Lat.	Lon.	Elev. (m)	Network	Start	End	In Park?
Ulupalakua Ranch 250	20.652	-156.401	579	COOP	1/1/1955	Present	NO
Wahikuli 364	20.900	-156.667	0	COOP	M	Present	NO
Wahikuli 364	20.900	-156.666	177	COOP	10/1/1949	11/1/2001	NO
Waiehu Camp 484	20.919	-156.513	98	COOP	9/1/1944	Present	NO
Waihee 483	20.933	-156.517	67	COOP	8/1/1916	4/30/1963	NO
Waihee Valley 482	20.947	-156.526	91	COOP	10/1/1949	Present	NO
Waikamoi 449	20.865	-156.193	366	COOP	10/1/1949	Present	NO
Waikamoi Dam 336	20.812	-156.233	1317	COOP	10/2/1949	Present	NO
Waikapu 390	20.852	-156.512	130	COOP	8/16/1916	Present	NO
Waikapu CC 390.4	20.838	-156.516	146	COOP	2/24/2003	Present	NO
Wailua Iki 348	20.800	-156.150	802	COOP	12/1/1971	2/1/1998	NO
Wailuku 386	20.900	-156.516	165	COOP	10/1/1949	11/1/2002	NO
Wailuku Ahos 386.6	20.890	-156.506	101	COOP	2/24/2003	Present	NO
Waiopai Ranch 256	20.634	-156.207	67	COOP	1/1/1905	Present	NO
AH6GR Maui	20.878	-156.519	265	CWOP	M	Present	NO
KH6HHG Makawao	20.855	-156.315	497	CWOP	M	Present	NO
Olinda Research facility	20.804	-156.285	1097	GPMP	6/13/1991	6/30/1995	NO
Hakioawa	20.580	-156.571	366	RAWS	9/1/2001	Present	NO
Kaneloa	20.522	-156.566	248	RAWS	9/1/2001	Present	NO
Lua Makika	20.563	-156.563	335	RAWS	9/1/2001	Present	NO
Kapalua W Maui Arpt. 462	20.966	-156.677	73	SAO	2/26/1987	Present	NO
Kahului Airport	20.900	-156.429	16	SAO	2/1/1944	Present	NO
Haleakala Summit 338	20.717	-156.267	3038	SAO	4/1/1957	Present	NO
Kailua 446	20.893	-156.215	213	SAO	9/1/1947	Present	NO
Hana Airport 355	20.797	-156.017	23	SAO	11/1/1950	Present	NO

Hawaii Volcanoes National Park (HAVO)

Name	Lat.	Lon.	Elev. (m)	Network	Start	End	In Park?
Halemaumau 52	19.405	-155.282	1110	COOP	10/1/1949	Present	YES
Kealakomo 38.8	19.295	-155.144	88	COOP	4/1/1995	Present	YES
Lae Apuki 67.12	19.317	-155.067	24	COOP	8/1/1989	2/20/1995	YES
Mauna Loa	19.483	-155.600	4103	COOP	M	12/31/1954	YES
Naulu Forest 38.6	19.317	-155.133	427	COOP	7/1/1965	1/1/1971	YES
Hawaii Volcanoes	19.420	-155.288	1123	GPMP	10/1/1999	Present	YES
Hawaii Volcanoes VC	19.431	-155.258	1215	GPMP	10/1/1986	Present	YES
Mauna Loa Observatory	19.539	-155.579	3399	OBOP	1/1/1955	Present	YES
Hairpin	19.318	-155.126	452	RAWS	2/1/2003	3/31/2003	YES
Keamoku Lava Flow	19.476	-155.363	1707	RAWS	2/1/1988	12/31/1998	YES
Keaumo	19.474	-155.359	1683	RAWS	2/1/1999	Present	YES
Kupu Kupu	19.348	-155.126	711	RAWS	2/1/2003	4/30/2003	YES
Pali 2	19.318	-155.292	848	RAWS	7/1/1999	Present	YES
Thurston Lava Tubes	19.420	-155.240	1199	CASTNet	10/1/1999	6/1/2004	NO
Ahua Umi 75	19.633	-155.783	1592	COOP	1/1/1958	12/5/1986	NO
Amauulu 89.2	19.733	-155.150	454	COOP	1/1/1953	1/14/1994	NO
Cape Kumukahi	19.517	-154.800	20	COOP	11/1/1957	1/20/1960	NO
Glenwood	19.483	-155.150	702	COOP	1/1/1916	12/31/1929	NO
Glenwood 54.2	19.511	-155.172	799	COOP	2/24/2003	Present	NO
Glenwood No 2 55.4	19.522	-155.144	671	COOP	3/1/2000	Present	NO

Name	Lat.	Lon.	Elev. (m)	Network	Start	End	In Park?
Hakalau 142	19.900	-155.133	49	COOP	1/3/1905	1/31/1994	NO
Hakalau Mauka 135	19.883	-155.167	351	COOP	10/1/1949	4/30/1963	NO
Halepiula 117	19.933	-155.400	1760	COOP	10/1/1949	12/31/1976	NO
Halepohaku 111	19.764	-155.459	2823	COOP	10/1/1949	Present	NO
Hapuu 31	19.433	-155.817	1391	COOP	10/1/1949	12/31/1952	NO
Ha's Farm 85.3	19.667	-155.100	177	COOP	2/1/1907	2/28/1978	NO
Hawaii Beaches 91.12	19.541	-154.912	88	COOP	9/1/1992	8/1/2005	NO
Hawaii Vol NP Hq. 54	19.433	-155.259	1211	COOP	10/1/1949	Present	NO
Haw'n Ocean View Est	19.122	-155.789	884	COOP	7/28/1980	Present	NO
Hilea	19.133	-155.533	101	COOP	1/1/1905	12/31/1939	NO
Hilo # 2	19.733	-155.067	0	COOP	M	Present	NO
Hilo 86a	19.733	-155.083	12	COOP	1/1/1905	7/31/1966	NO
Hilo A F 85	19.717	-155.083	12	COOP	10/1/1948	4/30/1963	NO
Hilo Country Club 86	19.683	-155.167	488	COOP	5/1/1970	3/1/1982	NO
Hilo International Arpt.	19.722	-155.056	12	COOP	10/1/1949	Present	NO
Honaunau 27	19.421	-155.884	287	COOP	1/1/1938	Present	NO
Honaunau No 2 27.6	19.466	-155.885	398	COOP	2/24/2003	Present	NO
Honohina 137	19.933	-155.150	91	COOP	4/2/1905	1/14/1994	NO
Honomalino 2.35	19.202	-155.862	610	COOP	2/1/1999	8/1/2002	NO
Honomu 136	19.867	-155.117	91	COOP	2/1/1994	8/1/1997	NO
Honomu Makai 143	19.867	-155.117	107	COOP	2/1/1994	11/30/1963	NO
Honomu Mauka 138	19.850	-155.150	335	COOP	5/1/1911	9/22/1993	NO
Kaala 123	19.933	-155.350	1666	COOP	10/1/1949	4/30/1963	NO
Kaala Iki 12	19.133	-155.567	409	COOP	10/1/1949	12/31/1978	NO
Kaawaloa 29	19.495	-155.919	409	COOP	1/1/1942	2/1/1999	NO
Kahiawai Mauka 3.8	19.133	-155.767	1257	COOP	2/1/1965	7/28/1980	NO
Kahuku Mauka 2.10	19.109	-155.747	957	COOP	5/1/2002	Present	NO
Kahuku Mill Camp 6.3	19.069	-155.681	668	COOP	2/1/1991	Present	NO
Kahuna Falls 138.2	19.861	-155.164	424	COOP	10/1/1993	Present	NO
Kainaliu Upper 73.29	19.531	-155.890	713	COOP	2/24/2003	11/1/2005	NO
Kaiwiki Homestead 89.11	19.753	-155.141	390	COOP	3/1/1999	Present	NO
Kalae	18.917	-155.683	12	COOP	12/12/1924	12/31/1949	NO
Kalapana 1 67.8	19.333	-155.033	3	COOP	7/1/1967	7/31/1989	NO
Kamaili 67	19.433	-154.933	0	COOP	1/1/1950	3/31/1955	NO
Kamaoa 2 5	19.033	-155.667	419	COOP	1/1/1958	5/1/1983	NO
Kamaoa 5	19.017	-155.667	336	COOP	12/1/1944	12/31/1952	NO
Kamaoa Puueo 5.1	19.014	-155.662	317	COOP	7/1/1983	Present	NO
Kanahaha 74	19.600	-155.800	1543	COOP	10/1/1949	4/30/1963	NO
Kaohe Makai 24.4	19.317	-155.883	37	COOP	1/1/1984	1/1/1995	NO
Kapapala Ranch 36	19.279	-155.454	652	COOP	10/1/1949	Present	NO
Kapehu Mauka 132.4	19.950	-155.217	335	COOP	9/1/1993	10/12/1999	NO
Kapoho 93	19.517	-154.850	0	COOP	1/1/1905	1/31/1960	NO
Kapoho Beach 93.11	19.504	-154.825	6	COOP	7/1/1975	Present	NO
Kapoho Landing 93.5	19.507	-154.866	88	COOP	5/1/1963	Present	NO
Kapoho Upper 66	19.500	-154.883	0	COOP	1/1/1950	7/31/1955	NO
Kapua 2.36	19.145	-155.849	534	COOP	8/1/2000	Present	NO

Name	Lat.	Lon.	Elev. (m)	Network	Start	End	In Park?
Kaueleau #2	19.433	-154.933	0	COOP	7/12/1907	12/31/1927	NO
Kauku 140.5	19.836	-155.151	457	COOP	9/1/1994	1/1/2001	NO
Kaumana 88.1	19.680	-155.143	360	COOP	1/1/1905	Present	NO
Keaau 92	19.636	-155.036	67	COOP	1/1/1905	Present	NO
Keaau Beach 91.13	19.646	-154.988	5	COOP	7/1/1996	2/1/2001	NO
Keaiwa Camp 22.1	19.239	-155.484	518	COOP	2/1/1965	Present	NO
Kealakekua 2 28.7	19.500	-155.917	442	COOP	1/1/1905	8/31/1977	NO
Kealakekua 26.2	19.495	-155.915	451	COOP	1/1/1905	Present	NO
Kealakekua 3 29.11	19.517	-155.917	466	COOP	5/1/1978	10/28/1986	NO
Kealakekua T F 29.12	19.521	-155.919	537	COOP	2/24/2003	Present	NO
Keanakolu 124	19.917	-155.350	1610	COOP	6/1/1905	5/31/1963	NO
Keanakolu Camp 124.2	19.922	-155.343	1610	COOP	2/1/1965	Present	NO
Keauohana 67.9	19.416	-154.955	232	COOP	12/1/1999	Present	NO
Kihalani 132.5	19.973	-155.239	302	COOP	6/1/1998	Present	NO
Kiolakaa 7	19.067	-155.617	320	COOP	1/4/1914	12/31/1953	NO
Kiolakaa A&F 6	19.067	-155.667	646	COOP	10/1/1949	12/1/1998	NO
Kiolakaa Keaa	19.067	-155.667	598	COOP	1/1/1970	Present	NO
Komakawai 30	19.400	-155.767	1877	COOP	10/1/1949	12/31/1952	NO
Kulani Camp 79	19.553	-155.304	1576	COOP	10/13/1947	Present	NO
Kulani Cone 81	19.533	-155.300	1563	COOP	7/1/1947	7/31/1950	NO
Kulani Mauka 76	19.586	-155.458	2530	COOP	7/4/1950	Present	NO
Kulani School Site 78	19.583	-155.333	1749	COOP	10/1/1949	8/20/1996	NO
Kurtistown 91.14	19.595	-155.084	293	COOP	8/1/1999	Present	NO
Laupahoehoe 133.1	19.988	-155.241	140	COOP	11/1/1993	10/1/2001	NO
Laupahoehoe PD 133.3	19.986	-155.236	125	COOP	2/24/2003	Present	NO
Lava Tree Park 66.1	19.483	-154.900	0	COOP	2/1/1965	11/30/1978	NO
Leilani Estates 67.1	19.450	-154.917	221	COOP	9/1/1982	11/4/1991	NO
Makahanaloa 2 134	19.817	-155.200	839	COOP	10/1/1949	12/31/1953	NO
Manuka 2	19.113	-155.829	537	COOP	10/2/1949	Present	NO
Mauka Reservoir 3.11	19.165	-155.699	1521	COOP	5/1/1983	Present	NO
Maulua 126	19.900	-155.317	1568	COOP	2/1/1921	7/31/1960	NO
Mauna Kea Observatory	19.817	-155.467	4199	COOP	7/1/1972	3/1/1982	NO
Mauna Loa Slope Obs. 39	19.539	-155.579	3399	COOP	1/1/1955	Present	NO
Milolii 2.34	19.210	-155.884	357	COOP	5/1/1985	Present	NO
Moaula 18	19.183	-155.500	183	COOP	10/1/1949	5/1/1983	NO
Mountain View #3 91.	19.533	-155.133	584	COOP	10/1/1990	12/1/1998	NO
Mountain View 91	19.553	-155.113	466	COOP	7/1/1906	Present	NO
Mountain View No 2	19.533	-155.100	482	COOP	11/1/1985	12/31/1989	NO
Naalehu 14	19.068	-155.592	244	COOP	1/1/1905	Present	NO
Napoopoo 28	19.472	-155.909	122	COOP	1/1/1905	Present	NO
Nauhi Gulch 128	19.867	-155.300	1556	COOP	1/1/1925	12/31/1953	NO
Ohia Lodge 24	19.267	-155.883	403	COOP	8/1/1948	6/30/1950	NO
Olaa Kurtistown	19.600	-155.067	198	COOP	1/1/1905	12/31/1926	NO
Opihihale 2 24.1	19.274	-155.878	415	COOP	5/1/1956	Present	NO
Orchid Ld Estates 91.5	19.567	-155.000	137	COOP	5/1/1963	10/1/1997	NO
Pahala 21	19.201	-155.480	256	COOP	1/1/1905	Present	NO

Name	Lat.	Lon.	Elev. (m)	Network	Start	End	In Park?
Pahala Mauka 21.3	19.207	-155.489	332	COOP	4/1/1985	Present	NO
Pahoa 65	19.518	-154.967	184	COOP	2/1/1905	Present	NO
Pahoa Beacon 91.9	19.544	-154.976	149	COOP	2/24/2003	Present	NO
Pahoa School Site 64	19.494	-154.946	208	COOP	1/9/1979	Present	NO
Pahoehoe	19.350	-155.883	305	COOP	9/1/1930	12/31/1947	NO
Pahua Mimi	19.417	-155.417	1568	COOP	1/1/1922	12/31/1936	NO
Pakao 37	19.367	-155.467	1525	COOP	10/1/1949	4/30/1978	NO
Papaikou 144.1	19.787	-155.096	61	COOP	1/1/1905	Present	NO
Papaikou Mauka 140.1	19.783	-155.133	392	COOP	10/1/1949	2/1/1990	NO
Papaikou Mauka No 2	19.796	-155.117	207	COOP	9/1/1993	Present	NO
Pepeekeo A F 140	19.833	-155.150	473	COOP	10/1/1949	6/30/1966	NO
Pepeekeo Makai 144	19.850	-155.083	31	COOP	10/1/1949	2/29/1972	NO
Piihonua 89	19.733	-155.167	528	COOP	10/1/1949	9/30/1981	NO
Piihonua Camp 5 88.4	19.717	-155.150	372	COOP	10/1/1981	10/1/1993	NO
Piihonua Kpua 89.11	19.718	-155.137	262	COOP	2/24/2003	Present	NO
Pohakuloa 107	19.753	-155.529	1985	COOP	10/1/1949	Present	NO
Pohakupuka 132.3	19.955	-155.188	82	COOP	8/1/1993	Present	NO
Puakala	19.783	-155.333	1923	COOP	1/1/1919	12/31/1935	NO
Puna Macadamia 91.11	19.619	-155.087	244	COOP	1/1/1992	Present	NO
Puu Kihe 120	19.900	-155.400	2365	COOP	10/1/1949	12/31/1976	NO
Puu Laau 102.1	19.833	-155.600	2270	COOP	10/1/1949	12/31/1976	NO
Puu Lehua 73	19.567	-155.817	1488	COOP	10/1/1949	12/5/1986	NO
Puu Loa	19.983	-155.333	763	COOP	1/1/1919	12/31/1926	NO
Puu Mali 113	19.917	-155.433	2123	COOP	10/1/1949	12/31/1976	NO
Puu Oo 82	19.733	-155.383	1934	COOP	1/1/1912	10/1/1975	NO
Puuhonua-O-Hona 27.4	19.421	-155.914	5	COOP	11/1/1970	Present	NO
S Glenwood 91.8	19.463	-155.114	628	COOP	5/1/1980	12/1/2003	NO
Saddle Road 1 84	19.700	-155.200	714	COOP	10/1/1949	4/30/1978	NO
Sea Mountain 12.15	19.137	-155.514	24	COOP	6/1/1982	Present	NO
South Kona 2 2.32	19.108	-155.789	720	COOP	6/1/1989	Present	NO
South Kona 2.31	19.100	-155.750	823	COOP	1/1/1977	5/1/1989	NO
South Point 5.2	18.993	-155.668	291	COOP	12/4/2003	Present	NO
South Point Corral 3	18.950	-155.683	153	COOP	1/1/1950	4/30/1978	NO
South Point Tracking	18.950	-155.683	93	COOP	2/11/1965	11/6/1969	NO
Stone Corral 115	19.950	-155.417	1598	COOP	10/1/1949	4/30/1963	NO
Volcano Observatory	19.433	-155.250	1211	COOP	M	Present	NO
Waiakea 88	19.633	-155.167	586	COOP	7/1/1942	12/31/1952	NO
Waiakea Mill	19.700	-155.067	15	COOP	1/1/1905	12/31/1948	NO
Waiakea SCD 88.2	19.661	-155.135	320	COOP	1/1/1953	Present	NO
Waiakea Uka 85.2	19.661	-155.130	305	COOP	2/24/2003	Present	NO
Wailea 137.4	19.888	-155.125	61	COOP	2/1/2004	Present	NO
Mauna Loa 5 NNE Hawaii	19.535	-155.576	3408	CRN	M	M	NO
Hilo 5 S Hawaii	19.645	-155.083	190	CRN	M	M	NO
CW0685 Naalehu	19.035	-155.631	280	CWOP	M	Present	NO
CW1949 Kamuela	20.085	-155.850	200	CWOP	M	Present	NO
CW3174 Hawi	20.237	-155.830	195	CWOP	M	Present	NO

Name	Lat.	Lon.	Elev. (m)	Network	Start	End	In Park?
CW3644 Hawi	20.214	-155.838	378	CWOP	M	Present	NO
CW4630 Pahoa	19.462	-154.928	261	CWOP	M	Present	NO
Upolu Point	20.250	-155.880	60	GPSMET	M	Present	NO
Mauna Loa	19.540	-155.580	3403	GPSMET	M	Present	NO
Hilo	19.720	-155.050	11	GPSMET	M	Present	NO
Pahoa	19.520	-154.960	180	GPSMET	M	Present	NO
Kaloko-Honokohau	19.673	-156.020	8	RAWS	12/1/2004	Present	NO
Puu Waawaa	19.795	-155.845	709	RAWS	4/1/2003	Present	NO
Puuanahulu	19.833	-155.770	831	RAWS	4/1/2003	Present	NO
Puuanahulu	19.833	-155.770	831	RAWS	4/1/2002	5/31/2003	NO
PTA Kipuka Alala	19.667	-155.708	1642	RAWS	8/1/1999	Present	NO
PTA West	19.772	-155.702	1308	RAWS	8/1/1999	Present	NO
PTA Portable	19.746	-155.627	1756	RAWS	5/1/2000	Present	NO
PTA Range 17	19.746	-155.626	1735	RAWS	4/1/2004	Present	NO
PTA East	19.683	-155.545	1960	RAWS	7/1/1999	7/31/2005	NO
Hakalau	19.821	-155.331	20	RAWS	4/1/2002	Present	NO
Hilo International Arpt.	19.722	-155.056	12	SAO	10/1/1949	Present	NO
Morse Field AAF	18.917	-155.683	12	WBAN	1/1/1940	12/31/1941	NO
Lyman Field AAF	19.717	-155.067	11	WBAN	4/1/1943	12/31/1945	NO
Hilo NAS	19.717	-155.050	12	WBAN	4/1/1944	12/31/1945	NO

Kaloko-Honokohau National Historical Park (KAHO)

Name	Lat.	Lon.	Elev. (m)	Network	Start	End	In Park?
Honokohau Harbor 68.14	19.679	-156.023	9	COOP	1/1/1991	Present	YES
Kaloko-Honokohau	19.673	-156.020	8	RAWS	12/1/2004	Present	YES
Holualoa 70	19.638	-155.914	982	COOP	1/1/1905	Present	NO
Holualoa Beach 68	19.617	-155.983	3	COOP	11/1/1928	2/28/1979	NO
Holualoa Makai 69.16	19.633	-155.967	317	COOP	7/1/1970	10/31/1976	NO
Honuaula 71	19.674	-155.880	1905	COOP	10/1/1949	Present	NO
Hualalai 72	19.698	-155.873	2354	COOP	10/1/1949	Present	NO
Huehue 92.1	19.757	-155.974	598	COOP	1/1/1905	Present	NO
Kailua	19.650	-156.000	0	COOP	M	12/31/1956	NO
Kailua Heights 68.15	19.617	-155.967	152	COOP	3/1/1979	12/1/1983	NO
Kailua Kona 68.3	19.650	-156.017	9	COOP	3/1/1956	2/1/1999	NO
Kalaoa 69.22	19.733	-155.983	610	COOP	6/1/1975	2/20/1986	NO
Ke-Ahole Point 68.13	19.731	-156.062	6	COOP	2/1/1981	Present	NO
Keauhou 2 73a	19.567	-155.933	589	COOP	12/1/1927	11/30/1956	NO
Kona Airport 68.3	19.650	-156.017	9	COOP	10/4/1949	8/13/1981	NO
Kona Village 93.8	19.833	-155.987	6	COOP	5/1/1968	Present	NO
Lanihau 68.2	19.667	-155.967	466	COOP	1/1/1950	Present	NO
Mahaiula 92.7	19.762	-155.995	293	COOP	6/1/1986	Present	NO
Middle Holualoa 68.1	19.617	-155.967	145	COOP	3/1/1958	2/1/1979	NO
Moanuiahea 69.24	19.742	-155.959	860	COOP	6/1/1986	Present	NO
Puu Anahulu 93a	19.817	-155.850	656	COOP	1/1/1950	4/30/1963	NO
Puu Waawaa 94.1	19.781	-155.846	768	COOP	10/1/1949	Present	NO
Waiaha Stream 70.16	19.636	-155.951	470	COOP	2/24/2003	Present	NO
Waikoloa Beach Rt. 95.9	19.913	-155.878	24	COOP	9/1/1989	Present	NO
Puu Waawaa	19.795	-155.845	709	RAWS	4/1/2003	Present	NO

Name	Lat.	Lon.	Elev. (m)	Network	Start	End	In Park?
Kailua Kona 68.3	19.650	-156.017	9	SAO	3/1/1956	2/1/1999	NO
Kailua Kona Ke-Ahole Ap.	19.736	-156.049	13	SAO	8/1/1970	Present	NO
Kona	19.650	-156.017	6	SAO	9/1/1947	Present	NO
Kalaupapa National Historical Park (KALA)							
Kalaupapa 563	21.190	-156.983	9	COOP	1/4/1933	Present	YES
Kalawao	21.183	-156.950	21	COOP	2/1/1905	12/31/1932	YES
Waikolu 540	21.130	-156.918	1082	COOP	4/1/1965	Present	YES
Makapulapai	21.203	-156.966	23	RAWS	3/1/1993	Present	YES
Puu Alii West	21.130	-156.917	1013	RAWS	3/1/1993	8/31/1997	YES
Waikolu Valley	21.142	-156.922	152	RAWS	3/1/1993	4/30/1999	YES
Halawa Valley 542.9	21.157	-156.742	3	COOP	1/1/1905	1/1/1998	NO
Hoolehua 559a	21.183	-157.050	256	COOP	6/16/1926	9/30/1955	NO
Hoolehua CPC 556	21.167	-157.117	128	COOP	10/1/1949	4/30/1963	NO
Kamalo 542.10	21.052	-156.871	6	COOP	4/1/1923	Present	NO
Kamalo Mauka 542.6	21.067	-156.867	18	COOP	6/1/1965	8/31/1970	NO
Kanepuu 690	20.881	-156.993	503	COOP	1/1/1955	Present	NO
Kaumalapau Harbor 65	20.790	-156.994	9	COOP	5/1/1963	Present	NO
Kaunakakai	21.100	-157.033	0	COOP	M	Present	NO
Kaunakakai 536	21.087	-157.023	4	COOP	1/1/1955	Present	NO
Kaunakakai Mau 536.5	21.095	-157.018	21	COOP	4/1/1965	Present	NO
Keonelele Pens 551	21.194	-157.205	171	COOP	4/1/1964	6/19/1997	NO
Kepuhi Sheraton 550.2	21.183	-157.246	43	COOP	4/1/1999	Present	NO
Kipu 562	21.167	-157.017	375	COOP	7/1/1942	4/30/1963	NO
Koele 693	20.833	-156.917	534	COOP	5/1/1911	4/30/1963	NO
Kualapuu 534	21.154	-157.037	252	COOP	5/1/1905	Present	NO
Lanai Airport 656	20.793	-156.953	396	COOP	10/1/1949	Present	NO
Lanai City 672	20.829	-156.920	494	COOP	1/3/1930	Present	NO
Lanaihale 684	20.817	-156.877	1027	COOP	5/1/1963	7/24/2005	NO
Mahana 694	20.866	-156.914	470	COOP	1/1/1955	Present	NO
Malauea 676	20.764	-156.911	351	COOP	5/1/1963	Present	NO
Mapulehu 542	21.067	-156.800	6	COOP	3/1/1921	1/27/1975	NO
Mauna Loa 511	21.133	-157.213	311	COOP	10/1/1949	Present	NO
Molokai Kaunakakai Molokai Airport	21.155	-157.095	137	COOP	10/1/1949	Present	NO
Pukoo 545.1	21.083	-156.800	3	COOP	8/1/1970	9/30/1976	NO
Puu-O-Hoku RCH 542.1	21.144	-156.735	213	COOP	1/1/1955	Present	NO
Waiakeakua 685	20.788	-156.874	610	COOP	1/1/1955	Present	NO
Lanai 1	20.873	-157.006	387	RAWS	4/1/2003	Present	NO
Molokai 1	21.115	-156.948	833	RAWS	4/1/2003	8/31/2005	NO
Puuhoikaweea	21.131	-156.875	256	RAWS	12/1/1994	8/31/1997	NO
Lanai Airport 656	20.793	-156.953	396	SAO	10/1/1946	Present	NO
Molokai Kaunakakai Molokai Airport	21.155	-157.095	137	SAO	1/1/1940	Present	NO
Puukohola Heiau National Historic Site (PUHE)							
Puukohola Heiau 98.1	20.030	-155.823	43	COOP	12/1/1976	Present	YES
Alakahi Lower 194	20.083	-155.650	256	COOP	1/1/1919	4/30/1963	NO

Name	Lat.	Lon.	Elev. (m)	Network	Start	End	In Park?
Alakahi Upper	20.067	-155.667	1214	COOP	1/1/1919	12/31/1948	NO
Awini 182.1	20.167	-155.717	570	COOP	1/1/1905	1/27/1975	NO
East Honokane 183.2	20.117	-155.717	1293	COOP	10/1/1949	1/27/1975	NO
Hawi 168	20.244	-155.841	177	COOP	1/1/1905	Present	NO
Homestead Plantation	20.217	-155.833	412	COOP	1/1/1919	12/31/1929	NO
Honokane 181.1	20.150	-155.733	244	COOP	11/1/1905	1/27/1975	NO
Kaauhuhu	20.200	-155.833	549	COOP	5/1/1985	2/11/1987	NO
Kahua Ranch HQ 176.3	20.128	-155.791	988	COOP	2/24/2003	Present	NO
Kamakoa 192.6	19.967	-155.683	766	COOP	5/29/1991	10/26/2000	NO
Kamuela 1 201.2	20.043	-155.611	878	COOP	2/24/2003	Present	NO
Kamuela 192.2	20.017	-155.667	814	COOP	10/6/1949	4/15/1980	NO
Kamuela Upper 192.7	20.035	-155.670	927	COOP	2/24/2003	Present	NO
Kaukini 184a	20.167	-155.700	610	COOP	7/1/1942	4/30/1963	NO
Kawaihae 98.2	20.033	-155.833	9	COOP	7/1/1963	Present	NO
Kawaihae Terminal	20.050	-155.833	3	COOP	5/1/1962	Present	NO
Kawainui Lower 193	20.083	-155.650	329	COOP	1/1/1919	9/21/1994	NO
Kawainui Upper	20.083	-155.683	1244	COOP	1/1/1919	12/31/1948	NO
Kehena 181.2	20.117	-155.750	1171	COOP	7/1/1942	9/30/1975	NO
Kehena Reservoir 176	20.167	-155.800	769	COOP	7/1/1942	4/30/1968	NO
Kohala 179.1	20.233	-155.783	95	COOP	1/1/1906	3/31/1971	NO
Kohala Maulili 176	20.217	-155.783	293	COOP	7/1/1942	9/30/1975	NO
Kohala Mission 175.1	20.229	-155.796	165	COOP	1/1/1905	Present	NO
Koiawe Lower 196	20.083	-155.633	220	COOP	1/1/1919	9/21/1994	NO
Koiawe Upper	20.067	-155.650	1025	COOP	1/1/1919	12/31/1948	NO
Lalamilo F O 191.1	20.012	-155.680	797	COOP	5/7/1980	Present	NO
Mahukona 159	20.183	-155.900	3	COOP	4/16/1912	12/31/1955	NO
Makapala Nursery 181	20.183	-155.767	488	COOP	2/1/1925	5/31/1952	NO
Mauna Kea Beach 98	20.017	-155.833	31	COOP	6/1/1967	12/31/1969	NO
Middle Pen 147.1	20.105	-155.836	421	COOP	5/1/1965	Present	NO
Niulii 179	20.233	-155.750	24	COOP	1/1/1905	9/30/1975	NO
Pololu Lookout 179.3	20.207	-155.738	149	COOP	6/1/1997	Present	NO
Ponoholo Ranch 178.11	20.153	-155.815	762	COOP	8/1/2003	Present	NO
Puakea Ranch	20.233	-155.867	183	COOP	1/1/1905	12/31/1934	NO
Puako 95.1	19.983	-155.833	15	COOP	11/1/1939	1/31/1976	NO
Puu Kapu 192.1	20.033	-155.633	869	COOP	10/1/1949	6/21/1967	NO
Puualala	20.067	-155.617	854	COOP	1/1/1919	12/31/1948	NO
Puukapu 204.3	19.983	-155.600	988	COOP	4/1/1995	6/1/1997	NO
Puukapu Homestead 192.9	20.041	-155.637	927	COOP	6/1/2004	Present	NO
Puuokumau 167	20.200	-155.833	549	COOP	7/1/1942	3/31/1971	NO
Upolu Point Airport 16	20.267	-155.850	27	COOP	10/1/1949	1/31/1957	NO
Upolu Point USCG 159	20.250	-155.883	19	COOP	5/51/1956	12/31/1992	NO
Waikanonoula 178.6	20.133	-155.783	1168	COOP	2/1/1965	1/31/1977	NO
Waikii 100.00	19.864	-155.654	1415	COOP	2/24/2003	Present	NO
Waikoloa 95.8	19.922	-155.801	268	COOP	7/1/1975	Present	NO
Waikoloa Beach Rt. 95.9	19.913	-155.878	24	COOP	9/1/1989	Present	NO
Waima Lower 197	20.067	-155.633	299	COOP	10/1/1949	4/30/1963	NO

Name	Lat.	Lon.	Elev. (m)	Network	Start	End	In Park?
Waimea	20.000	-155.683	814	COOP	M	Present	NO
Waimea Kohala AP	20.000	-155.667	813	COOP	5/1/1953	Present	NO
CW1949 Kamuela	20.085	-155.850	200	CWOP	M	Present	NO
CW3174 Hawi	20.237	-155.830	195	CWOP	M	Present	NO
CW3644 Hawi	20.214	-155.838	378	CWOP	M	Present	NO
Upolu Point	20.250	-155.880	60	GPSMET	M	Present	NO
Upolu Point USCG 159	20.250	-155.883	19	SAO	5/1/1956	12/31/1992	NO
Waimea Kohala Airport	20.000	-155.667	813	SAO	5/1/1953	Present	NO
Parkers Ranch AAF	20.250	-155.750	793	WBAN	7/1/1941	10/31/1941	NO
Suiter Field AAF	20.250	-155.833	30	WBAN	8/1/1940	4/30/1941	NO
Upolu Point	20.250	-155.867	27	WBAN	4/1/1943	12/31/1961	NO

Puuhonua o Honaunau National Historical Park (PUHO)

Name	Lat.	Lon.	Elev. (m)	Network	Start	End	In Park?
Hapuu 31	19.433	-155.817	1391	COOP	10/1/1949	12/31/1952	NO
Honaunau 27	19.421	-155.884	287	COOP	1/1/1938	Present	NO
Honaunau No. 2 27.6	19.466	-155.885	398	COOP	2/24/2003	Present	NO
Kaawaloa 29	19.495	-155.919	409	COOP	1/1/1942	2/1/1999	NO
Kainaliu 73.2	19.537	-155.929	457	COOP	1/1/1939	Present	NO
Kainaliu Upper 73.29	19.531	-155.890	713	COOP	2/24/2003	11/1/2005	NO
Kaohe Makai 24.4	19.317	-155.883	37	COOP	1/1/1984	1/1/1995	NO
Kealakekua 2 28.7	19.500	-155.917	442	COOP	1/1/1905	8/31/1977	NO
Kealakekua 26.2	19.495	-155.915	451	COOP	1/1/1905	Present	NO
Kealakekua 3 29.11	19.517	-155.917	466	COOP	5/1/1978	10/28/1986	NO
Kealakekua 4 74.8	19.514	-155.924	433	COOP	7/1/2002	Present	NO
Kealakekua T F 29.12	19.521	-155.919	537	COOP	2/24/2003	Present	NO
Komakawai 30	19.400	-155.767	1877	COOP	10/1/1949	12/31/1952	NO
Napoopoo 28	19.472	-155.909	122	COOP	1/1/1905	Present	NO
Ohia Lodge 24	19.267	-155.883	403	COOP	8/1/1948	6/30/1950	NO
Opihihale 2 24.1	19.274	-155.878	415	COOP	5/1/1956	Present	NO
Pahoehoe	19.350	-155.883	305	COOP	9/1/1930	12/31/1947	NO
Puuhonua-O-Hona 27.4	19.421	-155.914	5	COOP	11/1/1970	Present	NO

USS Arizona Memorial (USAR)

Name	Lat.	Lon.	Elev. (m)	Network	Start	End	In Park?
Ahuimanu Loop 839.12	21.432	-157.837	73	COOP	1/1/1905	Present	NO
Aiea Field 625 761	21.417	-157.950	140	COOP	2/1/1948	7/31/1970	NO
Aiea Field 68 756	21.400	-157.967	61	COOP	2/1/1948	4/30/1963	NO
Aiea Field 764a	21.383	-157.933	37	COOP	3/1/1905	10/31/1963	NO
Aiea Field 86 766	21.383	-157.917	95	COOP	12/1/1939	1/31/1961	NO
Aiea Heights 764.6	21.395	-157.910	238	COOP	9/1/1982	Present	NO
Alawai Yacht Harbor	21.283	-157.833	0	COOP	M	Present	NO
Aloha Stadium Halawa	21.383	-157.933	12	COOP	10/1/1975	6/30/1981	NO
Aloha Tower 704.8	21.304	-157.863	15	COOP	3/16/2000	Present	NO
B Y U Laie 903.1	21.643	-157.932	6	COOP	1/1/1942	8/1/1999	NO
Beretania Pump Station 7	21.306	-157.853	6	COOP	1/8/1958	Present	NO
Black Point 717	21.267	-157.800	27	COOP	8/1/1919	6/30/1963	NO
Camp 84 807	21.428	-158.061	232	COOP	1/1/1956	Present	NO
Camp Mokuleia 841.16	21.581	-158.183	2	COOP	8/1/1981	Present	NO

Name	Lat.	Lon.	Elev. (m)	Network	Start	End	In Park?
Campbell In. Pk. 702.5	21.317	-158.117	3	COOP	7/1/1971	Present	NO
Coconut Island 840.1	21.434	-157.787	5	COOP	6/1/1957	Present	NO
Dowsett 775.4	21.337	-157.834	119	COOP	9/2/1983	Present	NO
Dowsett Highlands 78	21.350	-157.833	172	COOP	5/1/1965	9/2/1983	NO
Ewa Plantation 741	21.375	-157.992	6	COOP	1/1/1905	Present	NO
Fort De Russy	21.283	-157.833	3	COOP	1/20/1958	2/28/1958	NO
H S P A Exp. Stn. 707	21.300	-157.833	15	COOP	1/1/1899	6/30/1976	NO
Haiku Plantation 838	21.433	-157.817	37	COOP	1/1/1916	11/29/1983	NO
Hakipuu Mauka 886.8	21.504	-157.858	40	COOP	2/24/2003	Present	NO
Halawa Shaft 771.2	21.381	-157.904	52	COOP	4/1/1965	Present	NO
Hauula	21.617	-157.917	24	COOP	1/1/1924	12/31/1941	NO
Hawaii 724.11	21.300	-157.717	9	COOP	12/1/1928	4/30/1974	NO
Hawaii Kai GC 724.19	21.299	-157.665	6	COOP	9/1/1907	Present	NO
Heeia	21.433	-157.817	31	COOP	5/1/1906	12/31/1927	NO
Heeia 2	21.450	-157.817	0	COOP	9/1/1963	Present	NO
Helemano Intake 881	21.550	-158.000	387	COOP	1/6/1942	5/31/1979	NO
Helemano Reservoir	21.533	-158.033	314	COOP	1/1/1942	4/30/1963	NO
Hoaeae Upper	21.450	-158.050	217	COOP	2/1/1908	12/31/1948	NO
Hokuloa 725.2	21.391	-158.100	689	COOP	6/1/1965	Present	NO
Honolulu	21.317	-157.867	4	COOP	10/1/1949	12/21/1976	NO
Honolulu	21.283	-157.833	0	COOP	M	Present	NO
Honolulu Intl. Arpt.	21.322	-157.925	2	COOP	7/1/1946	Present	NO
Honolulu Kewalo Basi	21.283	-157.850	0	COOP	M	Present	NO
Honolulu Observ. 702.2	21.315	-157.999	2	COOP	7/1/1960	Present	NO
Insane Asylum	21.333	-157.867	9	COOP	1/1/1905	12/31/1929	NO
Kaena Point 841.3	21.561	-158.239	378	COOP	5/1/1972	Present	NO
Kahana 883	21.478	-157.885	244	COOP	8/29/1916	Present	NO
Kahuku 912	21.695	-157.980	5	COOP	1/1/1905	Present	NO
Kahuku Pump 2 907	21.700	-157.983	3	COOP	1/1/1909	4/30/1963	NO
Kailua Fire Station 791.3	21.396	-157.739	3	COOP	1/1/1959	Present	NO
Kaimuki 715	21.267	-157.800	37	COOP	1/1/1921	1/31/1953	NO
Kalama Valley 724.13	21.300	-157.683	24	COOP	6/1/1974	8/31/1977	NO
Kalihi Res. Site 777	21.374	-157.822	277	COOP	9/1/1914	Present	NO
Kamehame 724.7	21.304	-157.681	249	COOP	2/24/2003	Present	NO
Kaneohe 838.1	21.423	-157.801	18	COOP	1/1/1905	Present	NO
Kaneohe Bay MCAS	21.450	-157.783	3	COOP	1/1/1942	Present	NO
Kaneohe Mauka 781	21.417	-157.817	58	COOP	8/1/1928	7/1/1998	NO
Kaneohe MCAS	21.433	-157.767	0	COOP	M	Present	NO
Kaneohe Yacht Club	21.417	-157.767	0	COOP	M	Present	NO
Kapaka Farm 904.1	21.613	-157.915	3	COOP	6/1/1981	Present	NO
Kapaka Makai 905.1	21.600	-157.900	3	COOP	12/1/1966	6/30/1972	NO
Kapalama 773	21.339	-157.858	187	COOP	5/1/1922	Present	NO
Kawai Iki Intake 880	21.567	-157.983	360	COOP	6/1/1910	1/31/1975	NO
Kawaihapai 841	21.580	-158.190	12	COOP	1/1/1942	12/18/2001	NO
Kawailoa	21.617	-158.083	52	COOP	8/1/1916	4/30/1963	NO
Kawela Mauka 906.3	21.667	-158.000	320	COOP	5/1/1965	12/31/1969	NO

Name	Lat.	Lon.	Elev. (m)	Network	Start	End	In Park?
Keehi Marina	21.317	-157.900	3	COOP	M	Present	NO
Kemoo Camp 8 855	21.539	-158.086	221	COOP	6/1/1933	1/1/2001	NO
Kii-Kahuku 911	21.695	-157.977	5	COOP	3/1/1980	Present	NO
Koolau Dam 833	21.498	-157.970	354	COOP	1/1/1919	2/1/1999	NO
Kualoa	21.517	-157.850	6	COOP	10/1/1926	12/31/1941	NO
Kualoa Ranch 885.6	21.531	-157.851	66	COOP	9/1/1996	Present	NO
Kunia Substation 740	21.386	-158.036	98	COOP	2/24/2003	Present	NO
Luakaha Lower 782	21.350	-157.817	268	COOP	1/1/1905	4/30/1963	NO
Lualualei 804	21.421	-158.135	34	COOP	10/1/1949	Present	NO
Lualualei TR NL 803.	21.483	-158.133	458	COOP	12/1/1953	7/31/1976	NO
Luluku 781.7	21.388	-157.809	85	COOP	3/1/1916	Present	NO
Lunalilo Home	21.283	-157.700	12	COOP	8/11/1956	11/30/1971	NO
Makaha Country Club	21.478	-158.196	76	COOP	9/1/1997	Present	NO
Makaha Kai 796.1	21.467	-158.217	6	COOP	1/1/1948	3/31/1977	NO
Makaha Mauka 842	21.517	-158.183	412	COOP	1/1/1948	4/30/1961	NO
Makaha Pump 800.2	21.483	-158.200	122	COOP	3/1/1969	10/8/1987	NO
Makaha Valley 800.1	21.483	-158.200	49	COOP	1/20/1958	2/26/1969	NO
Makakilo 730.1	21.350	-158.100	92	COOP	2/1/1976	5/1/1981	NO
Makakilo Res. 6b 730.	21.333	-158.067	35	COOP	8/1/1981	11/30/1982	NO
Makapoo Light	21.317	-157.667	0	COOP	M	Present	NO
Manoa 712.1	21.326	-157.823	67	COOP	1/1/1905	Present	NO
Manoa H S P A 785	21.333	-157.800	153	COOP	1/1/1941	4/30/1963	NO
Manoa Lyon Arbor 785.2	21.333	-157.803	152	COOP	3/1/1975	Present	NO
Manoa Tun 2 716	21.328	-157.791	198	COOP	1/1/1942	Present	NO
Manoa Upper	21.333	-157.800	92	COOP	5/1/1915	12/31/1931	NO
Manoa Upper 785.1	21.333	-157.800	95	COOP	9/1/1973	3/31/1975	NO
Manoa Waena	21.317	-157.983	0	COOP	1/2/1923	12/31/1931	NO
Maryknoll School 707.4	21.301	-157.834	51	COOP	2/19/1997	1/16/1998	NO
Matsonia Drive 720	21.300	-157.783	250	COOP	1/1/1942	12/31/1961	NO
Maunawili 787.1	21.351	-157.767	120	COOP	2/24/2003	Present	NO
Maunawili Ranch	21.367	-157.767	76	COOP	1/1/1905	12/31/1944	NO
Mikilua	21.417	-158.150	18	COOP	1/1/1928	12/31/1947	NO
Mililani 820.6	21.465	-158.001	232	COOP	2/24/2003	Present	NO
Moanalua 770	21.347	-157.891	6	COOP	1/1/1905	Present	NO
Moanalua Strm. 772.5	21.374	-157.880	70	COOP	2/24/2003	Present	NO
Momilani 835.1	21.417	-157.967	101	COOP	3/1/1966	8/31/1977	NO
Mount Kaala 844	21.503	-158.149	1227	COOP	1/1/1933	Present	NO
Niu Valley 723.8	21.290	-157.735	43	COOP	2/24/2003	Present	NO
Nutridge 710	21.317	-157.817	275	COOP	1/1/1942	10/31/1960	NO
Nuuanu Res. 4 783	21.353	-157.808	320	COOP	1/1/1938	Present	NO
Nuuanu Res. 5 775	21.339	-157.836	125	COOP	1/1/1905	Present	NO
Nuuanu Upper 782.3	21.350	-157.823	238	COOP	2/24/2003	Present	NO
Olomana Fire Station 790	21.378	-157.751	6	COOP	2/24/2003	Present	NO
Opaeula 870	21.579	-158.041	305	COOP	10/1/1949	Present	NO
Opaeula Lodge 870.1	21.567	-158.033	326	COOP	7/1/1974	5/20/1988	NO
P R I Dole Street 71	21.300	-157.817	24	COOP	10/1/1949	11/30/1956	NO

Name	Lat.	Lon.	Elev. (m)	Network	Start	End	In Park?
Pac Palisades 834.12	21.433	-157.933	323	COOP	9/1/1973	Present	NO
Paiko Drive 723.4	21.281	-157.734	3	COOP	5/1/1976	Present	NO
Palehua	21.400	-158.100	763	COOP	1/1/1922	12/31/1927	NO
Pali GC 788.1	21.373	-157.785	146	COOP	8/1/1944	10/9/2004	NO
Palisades Res. 835.2	21.430	-157.945	262	COOP	2/24/2003	Present	NO
Palolo Fire Stn.	21.299	-157.794	116	COOP	2/24/2003	Present	NO
Palolo Valley 718	21.323	-157.772	303	COOP	1/1/1942	Present	NO
Paradise Cove 726.1	21.345	-158.128	2	COOP	10/1/1999	7/1/2004	NO
Pauoa Flats 784	21.345	-157.806	500	COOP	10/1/1949	Present	NO
Pearl Country Club	21.393	-157.933	67	COOP	9/1/1977	Present	NO
Pearl Harbor NAS	21.350	-157.950	10	COOP	1/1/1941	12/31/1952	NO
Pearl Harbor Navy Ai	21.350	-157.967	15	COOP	1/1/1919	12/31/1940	NO
Poamoho Exp. Farm 855	21.538	-158.089	207	COOP	2/24/2003	Present	NO
Portlock Road 724.4	21.267	-157.717	9	COOP	1/1/1964	4/30/1976	NO
Pri Wahiawa 820.2	21.467	-158.017	214	COOP	6/1/1966	8/31/1976	NO
Punaluu Pump 905.2	21.584	-157.891	6	COOP	1/1/1913	Present	NO
Punchbowl Crater 709	21.310	-157.846	110	COOP	2/1/1950	Present	NO
Pupukea	21.650	-158.050	159	COOP	2/1/1906	12/31/1946	NO
Pupukea Farm	21.650	-158.050	198	COOP	1/1/1932	12/31/1946	NO
Pupukea Heights 896.	21.641	-158.036	229	COOP	7/1/1968	Present	NO
Puu Manawahua 725.6	21.381	-158.120	510	COOP	1/1/1977	7/24/2005	NO
Puuloa	21.350	-157.967	6	COOP	1/1/1919	12/31/1940	NO
St Stephen's Seminary	21.367	-157.779	137	COOP	10/1/1949	Present	NO
Tantalus 2 780.5	21.328	-157.824	405	COOP	1/1/1964	Present	NO
Tantalus 714	21.333	-157.817	400	COOP	1/1/1936	3/31/1957	NO
Tantalus Mauka	21.333	-157.833	488	COOP	8/1/1957	9/30/1962	NO
Tantalus Peak 780	21.333	-157.817	610	COOP	5/1/1965	1/31/1977	NO
U S Magnetic Observatory	21.300	-158.100	3	COOP	1/1/1905	6/30/1960	NO
U S Naval Station	21.300	-157.867	3	COOP	1/1/1905	12/31/1937	NO
Univ. Of Hawaii 713	21.300	-157.817	24	COOP	11/1/1925	Present	NO
Upper Wahiawa 874.3	21.503	-158.008	319	COOP	4/1/1971	Present	NO
Wahiawa 872	21.500	-158.033	281	COOP	2/1/1905	12/31/1965	NO
Wahiawa Dam 863	21.497	-158.050	260	COOP	1/1/1940	Present	NO
Wahiawa Mauka Intake 88	21.517	-157.950	369	COOP	10/1/1949	12/31/1965	NO
Waiahole 837	21.474	-157.884	227	COOP	1/1/1942	Present	NO
Waialae-Kahala 715	21.273	-157.780	3	COOP	2/1/1953	Present	NO
Waialee 896.3	21.683	-158.033	9	COOP	12/1/1971	10/31/1979	NO
Waialua 847	21.574	-158.121	10	COOP	1/1/1908	Present	NO
Waianae 798	21.441	-158.179	8	COOP	2/1/1905	Present	NO
Waianae 803	21.483	-158.150	482	COOP	10/1/1949	5/6/1974	NO
Waianae Kaiwiwi 801.	21.457	-158.180	12	COOP	2/24/2003	Present	NO
Waianae Valley 802	21.467	-158.167	101	COOP	10/1/1949	4/30/1963	NO
Waiawa 836	21.463	-157.933	244	COOP	10/1/1949	Present	NO
Waiawa CF 834.13	21.443	-157.959	235	COOP	2/24/2003	Present	NO
Waihee 837.5	21.451	-157.850	34	COOP	12/1/1986	Present	NO
Waihee Pump 839.8	21.446	-157.858	60	COOP	2/24/2003	Present	NO

Name	Lat.	Lon.	Elev. (m)	Network	Start	End	In Park?
Waikane 885	21.500	-157.883	232	COOP	1/1/1921	11/22/1982	NO
Waikiki 717.2	21.272	-157.818	3	COOP	1/1/1965	Present	NO
Wailupe Mauka	21.300	-157.767	61	COOP	1/1/1926	12/31/1937	NO
Wailupe Reservoir 72	21.300	-157.750	52	COOP	10/1/1949	12/31/1969	NO
Wailupe Valley School 7	21.292	-157.753	55	COOP	4/1/1966	Present	NO
Waimanalo Exp. Farm	21.336	-157.712	18	COOP	1/1/1907	Present	NO
Waimanalo Nonokio 795.2	21.336	-157.711	37	COOP	2/24/2003	Present	NO
Waimea 892	21.626	-158.068	101	COOP	1/1/1915	Present	NO
Waimea Arboretum 892	21.636	-158.054	12	COOP	9/1/1983	Present	NO
Waipahu 750	21.388	-158.007	18	COOP	1/1/1906	Present	NO
Waipio	21.383	-158.000	15	COOP	M	Present	NO
Waipio Heights 824.2	21.420	-158.006	125	COOP	2/24/2003	Present	NO
Wheeler AAF 810.1	21.487	-158.028	250	COOP	1/1/1939	Present	NO
Wilhelmina Rise 721	21.299	-157.785	335	COOP	10/1/1949	Present	NO
Wilson Tunnel 777.3	21.377	-157.816	320	COOP	2/24/2003	Present	NO
CW0875 Honolulu	21.300	-157.798	201	CWOP	M	Present	NO
CW2561 Kapolei	21.348	-158.083	107	CWOP	M	Present	NO
CW3005 Honolulu	21.300	-157.775	390	CWOP	M	Present	NO
CW4405 Kailua	21.380	-157.728	2	CWOP	M	Present	NO
CW4553 Waipahu	21.396	-158.024	88	CWOP	M	Present	NO
CW4581 Kailua	21.383	-157.739	6	CWOP	M	Present	NO
U of HI Manoa	21.300	-157.820	65	GPSMET	M	Present	NO
Windward Lei	21.410	-157.810	77	GPSMET	M	Present	NO
Dillingham	21.572	-158.199	31	RAWS	4/1/2004	Present	NO
Kahuku Training Area	21.679	-157.989	182	RAWS	5/1/2000	Present	NO
Kawailoa Training Area	21.587	-158.013	388	RAWS	1/1/2004	Present	NO
Kii	21.688	-157.953	2	RAWS	8/1/2002	Present	NO
Makua Range	21.529	-158.226	6	RAWS	7/1/1999	Present	NO
Makua Ridge	21.543	-158.199	534	RAWS	7/1/1999	Present	NO
Makua Valley	21.526	-158.204	159	RAWS	7/1/1999	Present	NO
Schofield Barracks	21.495	-158.082	299	RAWS	7/1/1999	Present	NO
Schofield East	21.499	-157.993	381	RAWS	5/1/2000	Present	NO
Schofield Firebreak	21.509	-158.115	347	RAWS	5/1/2000	Present	NO
Waianae Valley	21.481	-158.155	292	RAWS	4/1/2003	Present	NO
Ewa Kalaeloa Airport	21.317	-158.067	16	SAO	6/1/1943	Present	NO
Hawaii Kai GC 724.19	21.299	-157.665	6	SAO	10/1/1949	Present	NO
Honolulu Intl. Arpt.	21.322	-157.925	2	SAO	7/1/1946	Present	NO
Kaneohe Bay MCAS	21.450	-157.783	3	SAO	1/1/1941	Present	NO
Pearl Harbor NAS	21.350	-157.950	10	SAO	1/1/1941	12/31/1952	NO
Wheeler AAF 810.1	21.487	-158.028	250	SAO	1/1/1939	Present	NO
Ewa	21.333	-158.050	10	WBAN	6/1/1942	8/31/1942	NO
Ewa MCAS	21.333	-158.050	20	WBAN	1/1/1936	2/28/1949	NO
Fort Kamehameha AF	21.317	-157.950	20	WBAN	2/1/1935	12/31/1936	NO
Fort Weaver	21.317	-157.983	0	WBAN	2/1/1935	1/31/1936	NO
Hickam AFB	21.333	-157.950	3	WBAN	7/1/1938	12/31/1974	NO
Kahuku AAB	21.700	-157.967	3	WBAN	10/1/1941	2/28/1946	NO

Name	Lat.	Lon.	Elev. (m)	Network	Start	End	In Park?
Kipapa Field AAF	21.450	-158.017	204	WBAN	6/1/1942	9/30/1945	NO
Luke Field AAF	21.367	-157.967	5	WBAN	8/1/1931	12/31/1942	NO
Mokuleia Field AAF	21.583	-158.200	5	WBAN	6/1/1942	11/30/1945	NO
Schofield Barracks ASC	21.500	-158.033	272	WBAN	4/1/1923	9/30/1936	NO

4.2.2. Guam and Saipan

No weather/climate stations are currently operating within AMME boundaries (Table 4.4, Figure 4.2). The SAO station at Saipan International Airport is the closest source of near-real-time automated observations for AMME. There is also a COOP station operated at this location. Both data records extend back to 1988 (Table 4.4), with high-quality data. Two other currently-operating COOP stations in the vicinity of AMME, "Capitol Hill 1" and "Tinian", have data records going back to 1994 and 1987, respectively.

The CWOP network also has a station currently operating near AMME (CW3141 Saipan Airport), which may provide an additional source of near-real-time weather data. However, the period of record and data quality for this station are not known at this time.

There is currently one weather/climate station operating on-site at WAPA. This is a COOP station (Agat), whose data record extends from 1978 until present (Table 4.4). The best source for near-real-time data comes from the SAO station at Guam International Airport, only a few kilometers east of WAPA. An additional source of near-real-time weather data may come from the CWOP station "CW4647 Tamuning". The SAO station at Guam International Airport is also the best source for long-term climate records, as the data from this site are available as far back as 1945. A COOP station is also located at Guam International Airport, with the same period of record as the SAO station (Table 4.4).

Table 4.4. Weather/climate stations for AMME and WAPA. Listing includes station name, location, and elevation; weather/climate network associated with station; operational start/end dates for station, and flag to indicate if station is inside park boundaries. Missing entries are indicated by "M".

Name	Lat.	Lon.	Elev. (m)	Network	Start	End	In Park?
American Memorial Park (AMME)							
Capitol Hill	15.217	145.750	205	COOP	8/1/1980	7/1/1986	NO
Capitol Hill 1	15.214	145.750	252	COOP	12/1/1994	Present	NO
Kagman Comm Center	15.183	145.717	46	COOP	1/1/1984	9/30/1984	NO
Saipan International Arpt.	15.119	145.729	66	COOP	11/1/1988	Present	NO
Saipan Loran	15.133	145.700	3	COOP	1/1/1954	10/14/1980	NO
Saipan No 2	15.217	145.733	152	COOP	2/1/1960	7/31/1962	NO
Tinian	15.000	145.633	82	COOP	10/1/1987	Present	NO
CW3141 Saipan Airport	15.119	145.730	65	CWOP	M	Present	NO
Isley Marshall Island	15.117	145.733	65	SAO	7/1/1944	1/31/1945	NO
Saipan International Arpt.	15.119	145.729	66	SAO	11/1/1988	Present	NO
Saipan Kobler Airport.	15.133	145.700	32	SAO	2/1/1945	11/30/1945	NO

Name	Lat.	Lon.	Elev. (m)	Network	Start	End	In Park?
Saipan Marshall Island	15.117	145.700	32	SAO	11/1/1945	6/30/1962	NO
Guam Kagman Point	15.167	145.783	72	WBAN	7/1/1944	10/31/1945	NO
Guam Marpi Point	15.267	145.817	47	WBAN	5/1/1945	8/31/1945	NO
Saipan Marshall Island	15.217	145.750	11	WBAN	12/1/1941	5/31/1951	NO
Tinian Marshall Island	15.000	145.633	76	WBAN	12/1/1944	2/28/1946	NO
War in the Pacific National Historical Park (WAPA)							
Agat	13.389	144.658	3	COOP	7/1/1978	Present	YES
Apra Harbor	13.456	144.667	14	COOP	4/27/1994	Present	NO
Fena Filter Plant	13.367	144.700	112	COOP	1/1/1954	Present	NO
Fena Lake	13.362	144.706	18	COOP	1/1/1980	Present	NO
Guam International Arpt.	13.484	144.796	77	COOP	9/1/1945	Present	NO
Hughes Farm	13.367	144.733	106	COOP	8/1/1959	7/2/1965	NO
Inarajan-NASA	13.311	144.736	85	COOP	8/1/1978	Present	NO
Mangilao	13.453	144.798	18	COOP	7/1/1970	Present	NO
Mangilao Uog	13.433	144.798	82	COOP	5/20/1994	Present	NO
Pirates Cove	13.352	144.767	3	COOP	12/1/2004	Present	NO
Piti	13.462	144.689	3	COOP	7/1/1978	Present	NO
Talofofo	13.365	144.739	76	COOP	9/1/1996	7/20/1998	NO
Talofofo Village	13.350	144.750	91	COOP	7/1/1965	6/30/1970	NO
CW4647 Tamuning	13.502	144.773	36	CWOP	M	Present	NO
Guam International Arpt.	13.484	144.796	77	SAO	9/1/1945	Present	NO
Guam Orote	13.433	144.633	30	WBAN	6/1/1945	5/31/1948	NO
Guam Orote	13.433	144.633	24	WBAN	12/1/1944	5/31/1948	NO

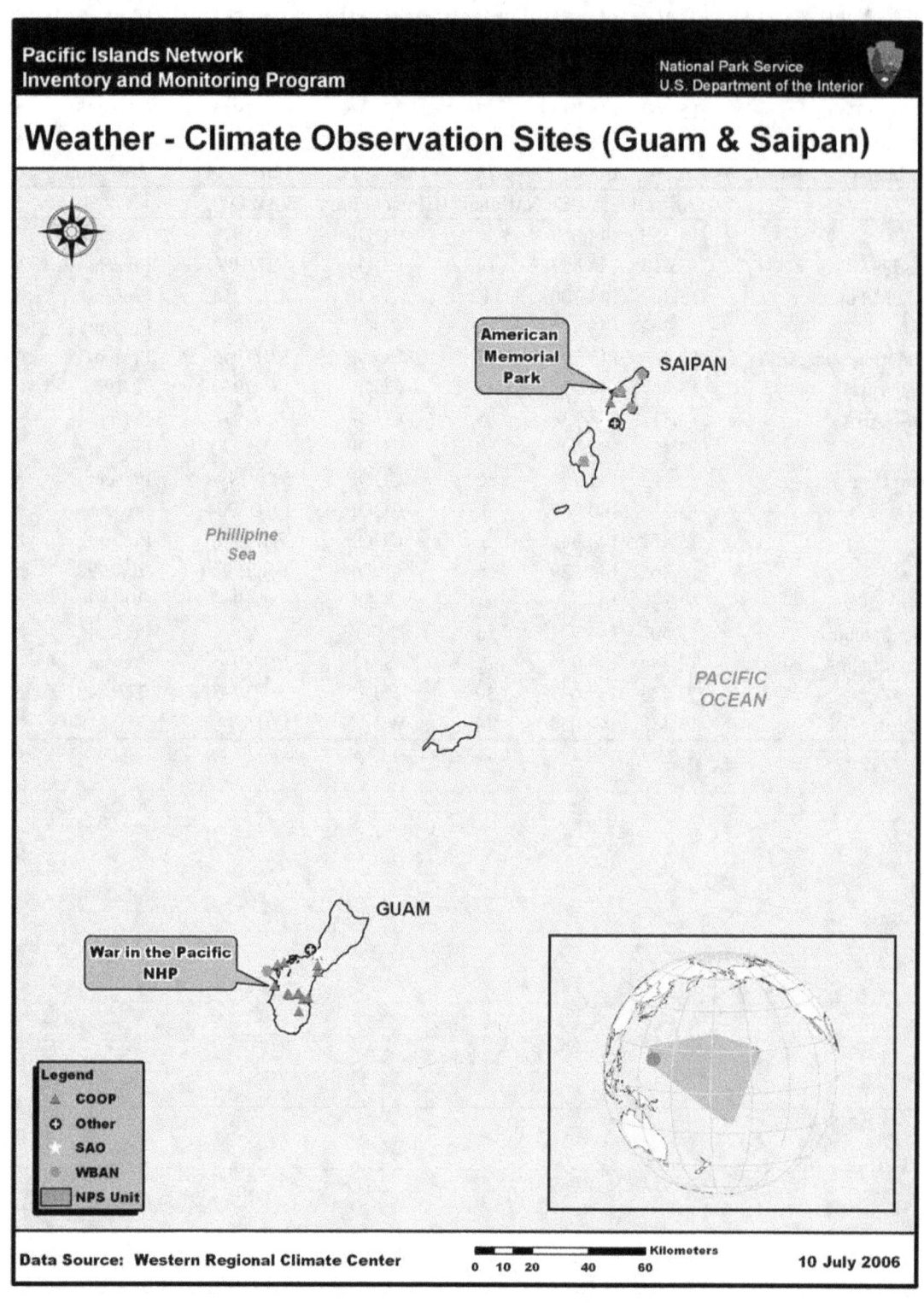

Figure 4.2. Station locations for AMME and WAPA.

48

4.2.3. American Samoa

There are no weather/climate stations currently in operation inside any of the NPSA park units (Figure 4.3, Table 4.5). Historically, there has been one station operated at a location which was to become part of NPSA. This was a COOP station (Vatia) that operated from 1948-1957. At present, there are only two automated stations near NPSA. One of these is the SAO station "Pago Pago WSO AP", about 5 km south of the NPSA unit on Tutuila. This SAO station has a data record extending back to 1956. A COOP station is co-located with the SAO station. The other automated station is an OBOP station, "Samoa Observatory", which has operated since 1974.

There are no active real-time sites on the Manua Group of islands (Figure 4.3). In fact, the only two climate stations presently operating on the Manua Group of islands are manual COOP stations (Ofu, Tau Airport). Data records from these two stations begin in the 1980s or later.

The longest data records for weather/climate stations on the islands of American Samoa extend back to the middle or late 1950s. The longest period of record is at the COOP site "Malaeloa", which has data starting in 1955. Besides Malealoa and the aforementioned COOP station "Pago Pago WSO AP", there are two COOP stations with periods of record starting in the 1950s (Table 4.5).

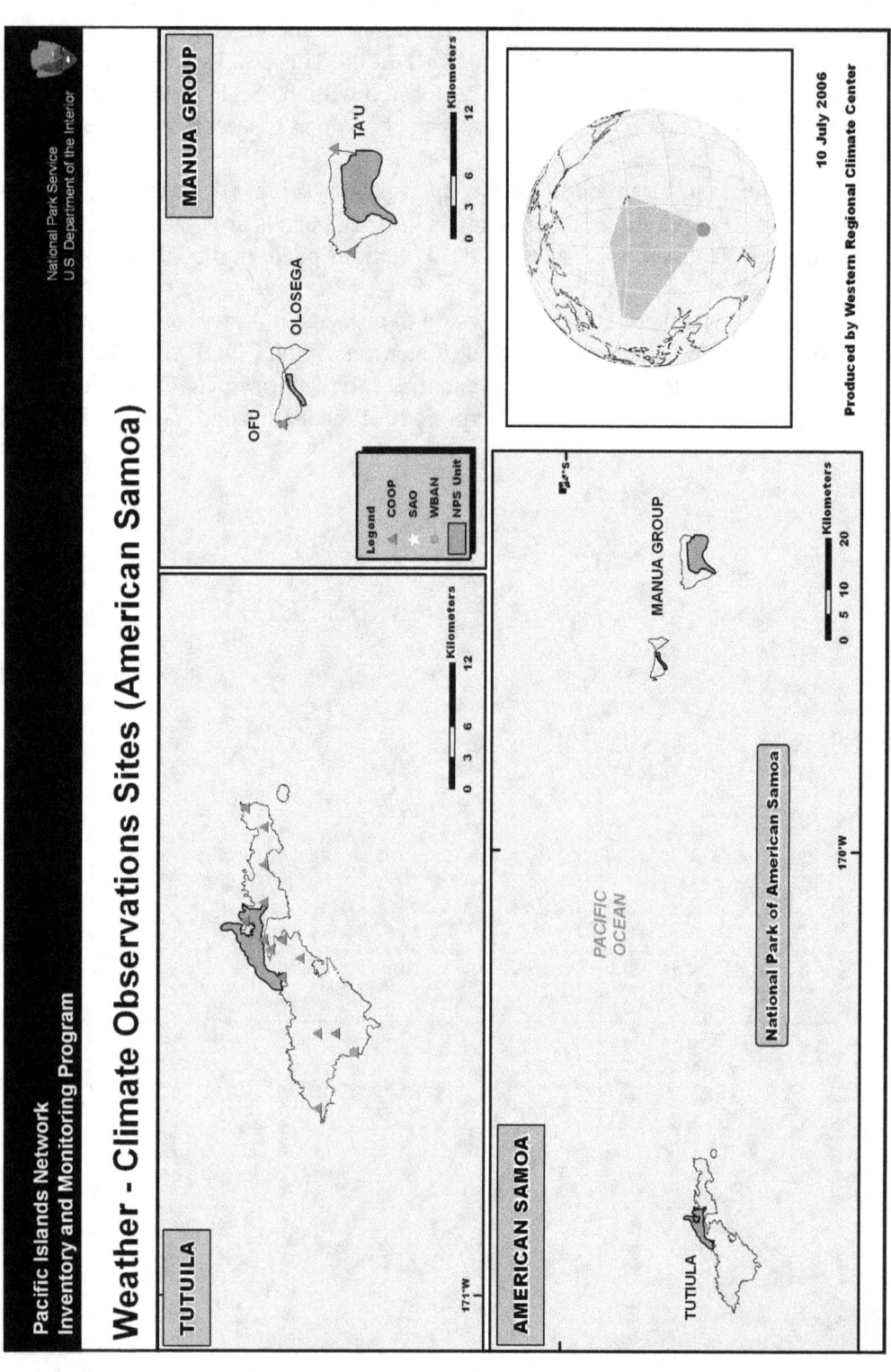

Figure 4.3. Station locations for NPSA.

50

Table 4.5. Weather/climate stations for NPSA. Listing includes station name, location, and elevation; weather/climate network associated with the station, operational start/end dates, and flag to indicate if station is inside park boundaries.

Name	Lat.	Lon.	Elev. (m)	Network	Start	End	In Park?
National Park of American Samoa (NPSA)							
Vatia	-14.250	-170.667	3	COOP	8/1/1948	3/31/1957	YES
Aasufou	-14.317	-170.767	409	COOP	1/1/1980	Present	NO
Afono	-14.267	-170.650	183	COOP	1/1/1980	9/22/1998	NO
Amouli Tutuila	-14.267	-170.583	6	COOP	4/1/1955	10/31/1957	NO
Atuu	-14.267	-170.683	81	COOP	10/1/1977	10/17/2000	NO
Cape Matatula	-14.250	-170.567	61	COOP	10/21/1991	Present	NO
Cape Taputapu	-14.317	-170.833	122	COOP	10/21/1991	Present	NO
Faga Alu Reservoir	-14.300	-170.700	250	COOP	9/1/1963	12/31/1977	NO
Faga Alu Stream	-14.283	-170.683	24	COOP	7/1/1958	5/31/1965	NO
Faga Togo	-14.283	-170.683	57	COOP	7/1/1958	Present	NO
Fagaitua	-14.267	-170.617	5	COOP	10/21/1991	Present	NO
Fagasa Tutuila	-14.283	-170.717	15	COOP	3/1/1957	9/30/1957	NO
Faleasao Village	-14.233	-169.517	5	COOP	11/1/1975	1/27/1987	NO
Leone	-14.350	-170.783	2	COOP	10/21/1991	Present	NO
Luma Village	-14.233	-169.517	6	COOP	7/1/1969	11/30/1974	NO
Malaeloa	-14.333	-170.767	42	COOP	4/1/1955	Present	NO
Ofu	-14.167	-169.717	3	COOP	6/1/1955	10/31/1957	NO
Ofu	-14.167	-169.683	5	COOP	10/10/1987	Present	NO
Pago Pago WSO AP	-14.331	-170.714	4	COOP	1/1/1956	Present	NO
Tau Airport	-14.217	-169.417	32	COOP	4/22/1991	Present	NO
Vaipito	-14.273	-170.692	81	COOP	7/1/1958	Present	NO
Samoa Observatory	-14.230	-170.560	77	OBOP	1/1/1974	Present	NO
Pago Pago WSO AP	-14.331	-170.714	4	SAO	1/1/1956	Present	NO
Tafuna American Samoa	-14.333	-170.683	3	SAO	5/1/1940	5/31/1950	NO
Leone Bay Amer. Samoa	-14.367	-170.783	21	WBAN	4/1/1962	7/31/1962	NO

5.0. Conclusions and Recommendations

We have based our findings on an examination of the available records and the topography and climate within PACN park units, discussions with NPS staff and other collaborators, and prior knowledge of the area. The PACN office has already been active in compiling lists of active weather and climate stations in their network, including those stations with HaleNet. The PACN network has also actively partnered with efforts to use PRISM (Parameter Regression on Independent Slopes Model) to document spatial variations in climatic elements, particularly precipitation, for the PACN islands. Here, we offer an evaluation and general comments pertaining to the status, prospects, and needs for climate-monitoring capabilities in the PACN.

5.1. Pacific Island Inventory and Monitoring Network

Metadata and data records for most of the weather and climate stations identified within the PACN are sufficiently complete and of satisfactory quality. The primary exceptions to this are for stations listed for the CWOP and GPSMET networks, where information was limited regarding contact information and station start dates.

There are numerous manual and automated weather/climate stations in the vicinity of the PACN park units on the Hawaiian Islands (Figure 4.1). With the exception of interior areas on the islands of Maui and Hawaii, manual stations are spaced only a few kilometers apart. Automated stations are spaced about 20-40 km apart throughout the islands.

The least dense coverage of weather/climate stations on the Hawaiian Islands is indicated for HAVO. Although sparse station coverage is also indicated in HALE (Figure 4.1), the HaleNet stations provide much needed weather and climate data for the park, as discussed in Chapter 4. In any case, great care must be taken to maintain the operation of any stations that are currently active. The records available from those stations located on or near the summit of Mauna Loa are particularly useful in tracking global-scale climatic changes, as this is a location that is widely noted for ongoing long-term climate monitoring efforts. In addition, it could be useful to re-activate some of those stations that have recently ceased operations in or near the HALE and HAVO park units. An example is the former CASTNet site near HAVO (Thurston Lava Tubes; see Table 4.3). Promoting active partnerships with agencies that run major weather/climate networks such as RAWS will further encourage the installation of weather/climate stations in areas that currently have little or no station coverage.

In fact, one area where such a partnership with the RAWS network could be profitable is the region surrounding PUHO. There are currently no automated sites that provide near-real-time data in the close vicinity of PUHO. The closest automated stations of any type are about 40 km away. By partnering with those agencies responsible for the RAWS network sites in Hawaii, installing a RAWS station on the west slopes of Mauna Loa would not only provide real-time weather conditions for PUHO, in a region where no such real-time observations are available, but could also benefit local fire management efforts. There are currently no RAWS stations across significant portions of the south and west sides of Mauna Loa. The south side of Mauna Loa is characterized by sparse vegetation and expansive fields of volcanic rock. However, a RAWS station could be particularly useful on the west sides of Mauna Loa, at lower elevations where vegetation is present and may occasionally be susceptible to fire conditions. This would also benefit weather and climate monitoring efforts for ALKA by providing much-needed real-time measurements for the southern portions of ALKA.

The PACN park units on the islands of Guam and Saipan (WAPA and AMME, respectively) have nearby manual COOP stations and automated SAO stations to work with. A RAWS station has been recently purchased by WAPA, with the intention of providing real-time weather conditions at the park. When installing new stations, care must be taken to ensure that the station is sited in an open, fairly level location that is representative of the surrounding area and is not located too close to trees, buildings, or other obstructions (WMO 1983). We examined potential locations for the WAPA RAWS installation, using aerial photos and topographic maps. The best sites from a climate representativeness standpoint would be the higher elevated locations of the Mt. Chachao / Mt. Tenjo Unit, or at Mt. Alifan. These sites appear to be free of trees and other obstructions to wind, with apparently lower vegetation. The Fonte Plateau is also elevated, but appears to have taller vegetation and trees, and perhaps standing water, which are both best avoided. One would like good exposure in all directions in order to track variations in the trade winds. Another advantage of elevated sites is reduced exposure to the corrosive effects of salt. There appear to be maintenance or visitor facilities that would be staffed at least occasionally with NPS personnel near these recommended sites.

In some cases, such as Guam International Airport, the COOP and SAO stations around WAPA and AMME provide several decades of reliable climate data. These types of stations are especially valuable on smaller islands such as Guam and Saipan, which cannot support the same number of weather and climate stations as can larger islands or mainland locations. Therefore, it is important that the NPS encourage local officials who are responsible for operating these stations to continue to maintain reliable observations. The climate records available from those stations are extremely valuable for tracking global-scale climatic changes.

Similar efforts must be encouraged for those active weather and climate stations on the islands of American Samoa. These islands are small enough that the NPSA park units can obtain representative weather and climate data from surrounding stations that are currently active. However, one concern for NPSA is the availability of real-time weather data for some of its units. The only known near-real-time observations are provided at the Pago Pago airport, on the island of Tutuila, and the American Samoa OBOP station. The NPSA units on Tutuila are separated from those on the Manua Group by over 100 km (Figure 4.3). Real-time observations from the Pago Pago airport on Tutuila cannot necessarily be expected to be representative of current conditions on the Manua Group. The present lack of any real-time information on the Manua Group islands may be detrimental for management of the NPSA park units on these islands. A likely candidate site for the installation of an automated station on Manua Group would be at Tau Airport, where an automated station such as RAWS or SAO (ASOS, AWOS, etc.) would be a useful complement to the manual COOP station that currently operates there. The NPS could benefit greatly by pursuing any opportunities to complete such an installation. In the meantime, it is important to retain of the active manual stations on the Manua Group. Although these stations are outside of the NPSA park unit boundaries, they are currently the only source of weather observations for the Manua Group islands.

5.2. Spatial Variations in Mean Climate

With local variations over short horizontal and vertical distances, topography and persistent trade winds are major controlling factors on the park units within the PACN, leading to systematic spatial variations in mean surface climate. This is particularly true for precipitation. Issues encountered in mapping mean climate are discussed in Appendix E and in Redmond et al. (2005).

If only a few stations will be emplaced, the primary goal should be overall characterization of the main climatic elements (temperature and precipitation). This level of characterization generally requires that (a) stations should not be located in deep valley bottoms or near excessively steep slopes and (b) stations should be distributed spatially in the major biomes of each park. If such stations already are present in the vicinity, then additional stations would be best used for two important and somewhat competing purposes: (a) add redundancy as backup for loss of data from current stations (or loss of the physical stations) or (b) provide added information on spatial heterogeneity in climate arising from topographic diversity.

5.3. Climate Change Detection

Due to influences from topography and trade winds, precipitation is more variable than temperature, both spatially and temporally, on the islands in the PACN. Not surprisingly, many of the weather/climate stations listed in this report, particularly manual stations with the COOP network, measure only precipitation. With the exception of variations with elevation, the tropical marine setting of the PACN ensures that temperatures throughout the PACN are fairly uniform. Temperature also varies little with time for the PACN. Although these stable temperatures are not as interesting for day-to-day weather observations, they do provide a useful indicator of longer-term global temperature trends. Temperatures in the PACN are regulated strongly by the Pacific Ocean, the heat content of which will respond to global-scale warming or cooling trends (IPCC 2001). Most of the PACN park units are located on the coasts of the PACN islands, which would be directly impacted by any sea level changes associated with global-scale temperature changes (IPCC 2001; Shea et al. 2001). Therefore, monitoring temperature characteristics for the PACN should be a high priority. Care should be taken to ensure the continued operation of any existing weather/climate stations that measure both temperature and precipitation. Long-term climate monitoring efforts in near-coastal marine ecosystems could be enhanced by installing weather buoys that monitoring not only atmospheric conditions but also oceanic parameters such as sea surface temperature.

The desire for credible, accurate, complete, and long-term climate records—from any location—cannot be overemphasized. Thus, this consideration always should have a high priority. However, because of spatial diversity in climate, monitoring that fills knowledge gaps and provides information on long-term temporal variability in short-distance relationships also will be valuable. We cannot be sure that climate variability and climate change will affect all parts of a given park unit equally. In fact, it is appropriate to speculate that this is not the case, and spatial variations in temporal variability extend to small spatial scales (a few kilometers or less in some cases).

5.4. Aesthetics

This issue arises frequently enough to deserve comment. Standards for quality climate measurements require open exposures away from heat sources, buildings, pavement, close vegetation and tall trees, and human intrusion (thus away from property lines). By their nature, sites that meet these standards are usually quite visible. In many settings (such as heavily forested areas) these sites also are quite rare, making them precisely the same places that managers wish to protect from aesthetic intrusion. The most suitable and scientifically defensible sites frequently are rejected as candidate locations for weather/climate stations. Most weather/climate stations, therefore, tend to be "hidden" but many of these hidden locations are inferior. Some measure of compromise is nearly always called for in siting weather and climate stations.

The public has vast interest and curiosity in weather and climate, and within the NPS I&M networks, such measurements consistently rate near or at the top of desired public information. There seem to be many possible opportunities for exploiting and embracing this widespread interest within the interpretive mission of the NPS. One way to do this would be to highlight rather than hide these stations and educate the public about the need for adequate siting.

5.5. Information Access

Access to information promotes its use, which in turn promotes attention to station care and maintenance, better data, and more use. An end-to-end view that extends from sensing to decision support is far preferable to isolated and disconnected activities and aids the support infrastructure that is ultimately so necessary for successful, long-term climate monitoring.

Decisions about improvements in monitoring capacity are facilitated greatly by the ability to examine available climate information. Various methods are being created at WRCC to improve access to that information. Web pages providing historic and ongoing climate data, and information from PACN park units can be accessed at http://www.wrcc.dri.edu/nps. In the event that this URL changes, there still will be links from the main WRCC Web page entitled "Projects" under NPS.

The WRCC has been steadily developing software to summarize data from hourly sites. This has been occurring under the aegis of the RAWS program and a growing array of product generators ranging from daily and monthly data lists to wind roses and hourly frequency distributions. All park data are available to park personnel via an access code (needed only for data listings) that can be acquired by request. The WRCC RAWS Web page is located at http://www.wrcc.dri.edu/wraws or http://www.raws.dri.edu.

Web pages have been developed to provide access not only to historic and ongoing climate data and information from PACN park units but also to climate-monitoring efforts for the PACN. These pages can be found through http://www.wrcc.dri.edu/nps.

Additional access to more standard climatologic information is accessible though the previously mentioned Web pages, as well as through http://www.wrcc.dri.edu/summary. These summaries are generally for COOP stations.

5.6. Summarized Conclusions and Recommendations

- Much work already has been done by the PACN to locate weather/climate stations.
- Climate characteristics within PACN, particularly precipitation, are highly variable spatially due to regional topography and trade wind influences.
- Station coverage is best for the Hawaiian Islands park units, particularly on the islands of Maui (for HALE) and Oahu (for USAR).
- For the island environments of PACN, it is important for NPS to support any attempts by local officials to continue the operation of active weather/climate stations, particularly those that have reliable, longer-term data records.
- There are currently no automated stations that supply real-time data at or near PUHO. Partnerships with the RAWS program may be advantageous to both NPS and RAWS, both for real-time weather information and for monitoring fire conditions.
- A RAWS station is planned for installation at WAPA. To maximize good exposure in all directions, potential sites should be elevated and include Mt. Chachao / Mt. Tenjo, Mt. Alifon, and Fonte Plateau.
- The NPSA park units on the Manua Group islands of American Samoa have no on-site real-time weather measurements. We suggest retaining the existing COOP site at Tau Airport and augmenting it with either a RAWS station or a SAO station.

6.0. Literature Cited

American Association of State Climatologists. 1985. Heights and exposure standards for sensors on automated weather stations. The State Climatologist **9**.

Andersson, A. J., F. T. Mackenzie, and L. M Ver. 2003. Solution of shallow-water carbonates: An insignificant buffer against rising atmospheric CO_2. Geology **31**:513-516.

Baker, R. H. 1951. The avifauna of Micronesia, its origin, evolution, and distribution. University of Kansas Publications, Museum of Natural History.

Bonan, G. B. 2002. Ecological Climatology: Concepts and Applications. Cambridge University Press.

Brown, B. E. 1996. Coral bleaching: causes and consequences. Coral Reefs **16 (Suppl.)**:S129-S138.

Bruijnzeel, L.A. 2001. Hydrology of tropical montane cloud forests: a reassessment. Land Use and Water Resources Research **1**:1-18.

Bureau of Land Management. 1997. Remote Automatic Weather Station (RAWS) and Remote Environmental Monitoring Systems (REMS) standards. RAWS/REMS Support Facility, Boise, Idaho.

Carter, L. M., E. Shea, M. Hamnett, C. Anderson, G. Dolcemascolo, C. Guard, M. Taylor, Y. He, M. Larson, L. Loope, M. LaShaunda, and G. Meehl. 2001. Potential consequences of climate variability and change for the US-affiliated islands of the Pacific and Caribbean. *in* J. Mellilo, A. Janetos, and T. Karl, editors. Climate Change Impacts on the United States: Potential Consequences of Climate Variability and Change. Cambridge University Press.

Cayan, D. R., M. D. Dettinger, H. F Diaz, and N. E. Graham. 1998. Decadal variability of precipitation over western North America. Journal of Climate **11**:3148-3166.

Cuddihy, L. W., and C. P. Stone 1990. Alteration of native Hawaiian vegetation: effects of humans, their activities and introductions. University of Hawaii Press, Honolulu, Hawaii.

Daly, C., R. P. Neilson, and D. L. Phillips. 1994. A statistical-topographic model for mapping climatological precipitation over mountainous terrain. Journal of Applied Meteorology **33**:140-158.

Daly, C., W. P. Gibson, G. H. Taylor, G. L. Johnson, and P. Pasteris. 2002. A knowledge-based approach to the statistical mapping of climate. Climate Research **22**:99-113.

Doggett, M., C. Daly, J. Smith, W. Gibson, G. Taylor, G. Johnson, and P. Pasteris. 2004. High-resolution 1971-2000 mean monthly temperature maps for the western United States.

Fourteenth AMS Conf. on Applied Climatology, 84th AMS Annual Meeting. Seattle, WA, American Meteorological Society, Boston, MA, January 2004, Paper 4.3, CD-ROM.

Environmental Protection Agency. 1987. On-site meteorological program guidance for regulatory modeling applications. EPA-450/4-87-013. Environmental Protection Agency, Office of Air Quality Planning and Standards, Research Triangle Park, North Carolina.

Finklin, A. I., and W. C. Fischer. 1990. Weather station handbook –an interagency guide for wildland managers. NFES No. 2140. National Wildfire Coordinating Group, Boise, Idaho.

Giambelluca, T. W., M. A. Nullet, and T. A. Schroeder. 1986. Rainfall atlas of Hawaii. Report R76. Water Resources Research Center, University of Hawaii. Honolulu, Hawaii.

Gibson, W. P., C. Daly, T. Kittel, D. Nychka, C. Johns, N. Rosenbloom, A. McNab, and G. Taylor. 2002. Development of a 103-year high-resolution climate data set for the conterminous United States. Thirteenth AMS Conf. on Applied Climatology. Portland, OR, American Meteorological Society, Boston, MA, May 2002:181-183.

Gray, W. M. 1968. Global view of the origins of tropical disturbances and storms. Monthly Weather Review **96**:669-700

Hay, J. E., A. G. Suarez, P. P. Wong, L. Briguglio, and S. Ragoonaden. 2001. Small island states, Chapter 17 *in* Climate Change 2001: Impacts, Adaptation and Vulnerability. Contribution of Working Group II to the Third Assessment Report of the Intergovernmental Panel on Climate Change. Cambridge University Press.

HaySmith, L., F. L. Klasner, S. H. Stephens, and G. H. Dicus. 2005. Pacific Island Network Vital Signs Monitoring Plan: Phase III report. National Park Service, Pacific Island Network, Hawaii Volcanoes National Park, Hawaii.

Herbert, D. A., J. H. Fownes, and P. M. Vitousek. 1999. Hurricane damage and recovery of a Hawaiian forest: effects of increased nutrient availability on ecosytem resistance and resiliance. Ecology **80**:908-920.

I&M. 2006. I&M Inventories home page. http://science.nature.nps.gov/im/inventory/index.cfm.

IPCC. 2001. Climate Change 2001: Impacts, adaptation and vulnerability. Contribution of working group II to the third assessment report of the Intergovernmental Panel on Climate Change.[McCarthy, J.J., Canziani, O.F., Leary, N.A., Dokken, D.J., White, K.S. (eds.)]. Cambridge University Press.

Jacobson, M. C., R. J. Charlson, H. Rodhe, and G. H. Orians. 2000. Earth System Science: From Biogeochemical Cycles to Global Change. Academic Press, San Diego.

Jenny, H. 1941. Factors of soil formation: A system of quantitative pedology. McGraw-Hill, New York, NY.

Karl, T. R., V. E. Derr, D. R. Easterling, C. K. Folland, D. J. Hoffman, S. Levitus, N. Nicholls, D. E. Parker, and G. W. Withee. 1996. Critical issues for long-term climate monitoring. Pages 55-92 *in* T. R. Karl, editor. Long Term Climate Monitoring by the Global Climate Observing System, Kluwer Publishing.

Kennedy, V. S., R. R. Twilley, J. A. Kleypas, J. H. C. Jr., and S. R. Hare. 2002. Coastal and marine ecosystems & global climate change: potential effects on U.S. resources. Pew Center on Global Climate Change.

Lawton, R. O., U. S. Nair, R. A. Pielke Sr., and R. M. Welch. 2001. Climatic impact of tropical lowland deforestation on nearby montane cloud forests. Science **294**:584-587.

Loope, L. L. 1998. Hawaii and Pacific Islands. Pages 747-774 *in* M. J. Mac, P. A. Opler, C. E. Puckett Haecker, and P. D. Doran, editors. Status and trends of the nation's biological resources, volume 2. U.S. Geological Survey, Reston, VA. Online. (http://biology.usgs.gov/s+t/SNT/noframe/pi179.htm) Accessed 3 June 2004.

Loope, L. L., and T. W. Giambelluca. 1998. Vulnerability of island tropical montane cloud forests to climate change, with special reference to east Maui, Hawaii. Climatic Change **39**:503-517.

Meehl, G. A. 1996. Vulnerability of freshwater resources to climate change in the tropical Pacific region. Water, Air, and Soil Pollution **92**:203-213.

Mittermeier, R. A., N. Myers, and C. G. Mittermeier, editors. 1999. Hotspots: Earth's biologically richest and most endangered terrestrial ecoregions. CEMEX and Conservation International. Online. (http://www.biodiversityhotspots.org/xp/Hotspots/resources/bibliography.xml) Accessed 5 July 2004.

Mueller-Dombois, D., and F. R. Fosberg. 1998. Vegetation of the tropical Pacific islands. Springer-Verlag, New York.

National Research Council. 2001. A Climate Services Vision: First Steps Toward the Future. National Academies Press, Washington, D.C.

National Wildfire Coordinating Group. 2004. National fire danger rating system weather station standards. Report PMS 426.3. National Wildfire Coordinating Group, Boise, Idaho.

Neilson, R. P. 1987. Biotic regionalization and climatic controls in western North America. Vegetatio **70**:135-147.

Oakley, K. L., L. P. Thomas, and S. G. Fancy. 2003. Guidelines for long-term monitoring protocols. Wildlife Society Bulletin **31**:1000-1003.

Olson, D. M., E. Dinerstein, E. D. Wikramanayake, N. D. Burgess, G. V. N. Powell, E. C. Underwood, J. A. D'Amico, I. Itoua, H. E. Strand, J. C. Morrison, and others. 2001. Terrestrial ecoregions of the world: A new map of life on earth. Bioscience **51**:993-938.

Orr, J. C., V. J. Fabry, O. Aumont, L. Bopp, S. C. Doney, R. A. Feely, A. Gnanadesikan, N. Gruber, A. Ishida, F. Joos, and others. 2005. Anthropogenic ocean acidification over the twenty-first century and its impact on calcifying organisms. Nature **437**:681-686.

Ostertag, R., F. N. Scatena, and W. L. Silver. 2003. Forest floor decomposition following hurricane litter inputs in several Puerto Rican forests. Ecosystems **6**:261-273.

Redmond, K. T., D. B. Simeral, and G. D. McCurdy. 2005. Climate monitoring for southwest Alaska national parks: network design and site selection. Report 05-01. Western Regional Climate Center, Reno, Nevada.

Sanderson, M. 1993. Prevailing Trade Winds: Weather and Climate in Hawai`i. University of Hawaii Press, Honolulu, Hawaii.

Schlappa, K. 2005. Supporting documents: air quality and climate report. *In* L HaySmith, F. L. Klasner, S. H. Stephens, and G. H. Dicus. Pacific Island Network Vital signs monitoring plan: phase III report. National Park Service, Pacific Island Network, Hawaii Volcanoes National Park, Hawaii.

Schlesinger, W. H. 1997. Biogeochemistry: An Analysis of Global Change. Academic Press, San Diego.

Shea, E. L., G. Dolcemascolo, C. L. Anderson, A. Barnston, C. P. Guard, M. P. Hamnett, S. T. Kubota, N. Lewis, J. Loschnigg, and G. Meehl. 2001. Preparing for a changing climate: The potential consequences of climate variability and change for Pacific Islands. Pacific Island regional assessment of the consequences of climate change and variability. A report of the Pacific Islands Regional Assessment Group for the U.S. Global Change Research Program. East-West Center, Honolulu, Hawaii.

Chu, P., and M. Nakashima. 2004. Reestablishment of the Hawaiian Islands' climatic divisions in support of NOAA's efforts. Hawaii State Climate Office, University of Hawaii at Manoa, Hawaii.

Stadtmueller, T. 1987. Cloud Forests in the Humid Tropics. United Nations University Press, Tokyo.

Tanner, B. D. 1990. Automated weather stations. Remote Sensing Reviews **5**:73-98.

Trewartha, G. T., and L. H. Horn. 1980. An introduction to climate. McGraw-Hill. New York, NY.

Tsyban, A. V., J. T. Everett, and J. G. Titus. 1990. World Oceans and Coastal Zones. Chapter 6 *in* W. J. McG. Tegart, D.C. Griffiths, and G.W. Sheldon, editors. Climate Change: The IPCC Impacts Assessment. Contribution of Working Group II to the First Assessment Report of the Intergovernmental Panel on Climate Change. Australian Government Publishing Service, Canberra, Australia.

Vecchi, G. A., B. J. Soden, A. T. Wittenberg, I. M. Held, A. Leetmaa, and M. J. Harrison. 2006. Weakening of tropical Pacific atmospheric circulation due to anthropogenic forcing. Nature **441**:73-76.

Vitousek, P. M., C. M. D`Antonio, L. L. Loope, and R. Westbrooks. 1996. Biological invasions as global environmental change. American Scientist **84**:468-478.

Whistler, W. A. 1992. Botanical inventory of the proposed Tau unit of the National Park of American Samoa. Cooperative National Park Resources Studies Unit Technical Report 83, University of Hawaii at Manoa, Department of Botany, Honolulu, Hawaii.

Whistler, W. A. 1994. Botanical inventory of the proposed Tutuila and Ofu units of the National Park of American Samoa. Cooperative National Park Resources Studies Unit Technical Report 87, Honolulu, Hawaii.

World Meteorological Organization. 1983. Guide to meteorological instruments and methods of observation, no. 8, 5th edition, World Meteorological Organization, Geneva Switzerland.

World Meteorological Organization. 2005. Organization and planning of intercomparisons of rainfall intensity gauges. World Meteorological Organization, Geneva Switzerland.

Appendix A. Climate-monitoring principles.

Since the late 1990s, frequent references have been made to a set of climate-monitoring principles enunciated in 1996 by Tom Karl, director of the NOAA NCDC in Asheville, North Carolina. These monitoring principles also have been referred to informally as the "Ten Commandments of Climate Monitoring." Both versions are given here. In addition, these principles have been adopted by the Global Climate Observing System (GCOS 2004).

(Compiled by Kelly Redmond, Western Regional Climate Center, Desert Research Institute, August 2000.)

A.1. Full Version (Karl et al. 1996)

A. Effects on climate records of instrument changes, observing practices, observation locations, sampling rates, etc., must be known before such changes are implemented. This can be ascertained through a period where overlapping measurements from old and new observing systems are collected or sometimes by comparing the old and new observing systems with a reference standard. Site stability for in situ measurements, both in terms of physical location and changes in the nearby environment, also should be a key criterion in site selection. Thus, many synoptic network stations, which are primarily used in weather forecasting but also provide valuable climate data, and dedicated climate stations intended to be operational for extended periods must be subject to this policy.

B. Processing algorithms and changes in these algorithms must be well documented. Documentation should be carried with the data throughout the data-archiving process.

C. Knowledge of instrument, station, and/or platform history is essential for interpreting and using the data. Changes in instrument sampling time, local environmental conditions for in situ measurements, and other factors pertinent to interpreting the observations and measurements should be recorded as a mandatory part in the observing routine and be archived with the original data.

D. In situ and other observations with a long, uninterrupted record should be maintained. Every effort should be applied to protect the data sets that have provided long-term, homogeneous observations. "Long-term" for space-based measurements is measured in decades, but for more conventional measurements, "long-term" may be a century or more. Each element in the observational system should develop a list of prioritized sites or observations based on their contribution to long-term climate monitoring.

E. Calibration, validation, and maintenance facilities are critical requirements for long-term climatic data sets. Homogeneity in the climate record must be assessed routinely, and corrective action must become part of the archived record.

F. Where feasible, some level of "low-technology" backup to "high-technology" observing systems should be developed to safeguard against unexpected operational failures.

G. Regions having insufficient data, variables and regions sensitive to change, and key measurements lacking adequate spatial and temporal resolution should be given the highest priority in designing and implementing new climate-observing systems.

H. Network designers and instrument engineers must receive long-term climate requirements at the outset of the network design process. This is particularly important because most observing systems have been designed for purposes other than long-term climate monitoring. Instruments must possess adequate accuracy with biases small enough to document climate variations and changes.

I. Much of the development of new observational capabilities and the evidence supporting the value of these observations stem from research-oriented needs or programs. A lack of stable, long-term commitment to these observations and lack of a clear transition plan from research to operations are two frequent limitations in the development of adequate, long-term monitoring capabilities. Difficulties in securing a long-term commitment must be overcome in order to improve the climate-observing system in a timely manner with minimal interruptions.

J. Data management systems that facilitate access, use, and interpretation are essential. Freedom of access, low cost, mechanisms that facilitate use (directories, catalogs, browse capabilities, availability of metadata on station histories, algorithm accessibility and documentation, etc.) and quality control should guide data management. International cooperation is critical for successful management of data used to monitor long-term climate change and variability.

A.2. Abbreviated version, "Ten Commandments of Climate Monitoring"

A. Assess the impact of new climate-observing systems or changes to existing systems before they are implemented.

"Thou shalt properly manage network change." (assess effects of proposed changes)

B. Require a suitable period where measurement from new and old climate-observing systems will overlap.

"Thou shalt conduct parallel testing." (compare old and replacement systems)

C. Treat calibration, validation, algorithm-change, and data-homogeneity assessments with the same care as the data.

"Thou shalt collect metadata." (fully document system and operating procedures)

D. Verify capability for routinely assessing the quality and homogeneity of the data including high-resolution data for extreme events.

"Thou shalt assure data quality and continuity." (assess as part of routine operating procedures)

E. Integrate assessments like those conducted by the International Panel on Climate Change into global climate-observing priorities.

"Thou shalt anticipate the use of data." (integrated environmental assessment; component in operational plan for system)

F. Maintain long-term weather and climate stations.

"Thou shalt worship historic significance." (maintain homogeneous data sets from long–term, climate-observing systems)

G. Place high priority on increasing observations in regions lacking sufficient data and in regions sensitive to change and variability.

"Thou shalt acquire complementary data." (new sites to fill observational gaps)

H. Provide network operators, designers, and instrument engineers with long-term requirements at the outset of the design and implementation phases for new systems.

"Thou shalt specify requirements for climate observation systems." (application and usage of observational data)

I. Carefully consider the transition from research-observing system to long-term operation.

"Thou shalt have continuity of purpose." (stable long-term commitments)

J. Focus on data-management systems that facilitate access, use, and interpretation of weather data and metadata.

"Thou shalt provide access to data and metadata." (readily-available weather and climate information)

A.3. Literature Cited

Karl, T. R., V. E. Derr, D. R. Easterling, C. K. Folland, D. J. Hoffman, S. Levitus, N. Nicholls, D. E. Parker, and G. W. Withee. 1996. Critical issues for long-term climate monitoring. Pages 55-92 *in* T. R. Karl, editor. Long Term Climate Monitoring by the Global Climate Observing System, Kluwer Publishing.

Global Climate Observing System. 2004. Implementation plan for the global observing system for climate in support of the UNFCCC. GCOS-92, WMO/TD No. 1219, World Meteorological Organization, Geneva, Switzerland.

Appendix B. Glossary.

Climate—Complete and entire ensemble of statistical descriptors of temporal and spatial properties comprising the behavior of the atmosphere. These descriptors include means, variances, frequency distributions, autocorrelations, spatial correlations and other patterns of association, temporal lags, and element-to-element relationships. The descriptors have a physical basis in flows and reservoirs of energy and mass, even if they we cannot be used to discern how they arise and how they work. Climate and weather phenomena shade gradually into each other and are ultimately inseparable.

Climate Element—(same as weather element) Attribute or property of the state of the atmosphere that is measured, estimated, or derived. Examples of climate elements include temperature, wind speed, wind direction, precipitation amount, precipitation type, relative humidity, dewpoint, solar radiation, snow depth, soil temperature at a given depth, etc. A derived element is a function of other elements (like degree days or number of days with rain) and is not measured directly with a sensor. The terms "parameter" or "variable" are not used to describe elements.

Climate Network—Group of climate stations having a common purpose; the group is often owned and maintained by a single organization.

Climate Station—Station where data are collected to track atmospheric conditions over the long-term. Often, this weather station operates to additional standards to verify long-term consistency. For these stations, the detailed circumstances surrounding a set of measurements (siting and exposure, instrument changes, etc.) are important.

Data—Measurements specifying the state of the physical environment that specifically do not include metadata.

Data Inventory—Information about overall data properties for each station within a weather or climate network. A data inventory may include start/stop dates, percentages of available data, breakdowns by climate element, counts of actual data values, counts or fractions of data types, etc. These properties must be determined by actually reading the data and thus require the data to be available, accessible, and in a readable format.

NPS I&M Network—A set of NPS units (typically 3–20) grouped by a common theme, typically by natural resource and/or geographic region.

Metadata—Information necessary to interpret environmental data properly, organized as a history or series of snapshots—data about data. Examples include details of measurement processes, station circumstances and exposures, assumptions about the site, network purpose and background, types of observations and sensors, pre-treatment of data, access information, maintenance history and protocols, observational methods, archive locations, owner, and station start/end period.

Quality Assurance—Planned and systematic set of activities to provide adequate confidence that products and services are resulting in credible and correct information. Quality assurance encompasses quality control.

Quality Control—Evaluation, assessment, and improvement of imperfect data by utilizing other imperfect data.

Station Inventory—Information about a set of stations obtained from metadata that accompany the network or networks. A station inventory can be compiled from direct and indirect reports prepared by others.

Trade Wind Inversion—Transitional zone in subtropical oceanic atmospheres where warm, dry air at middle and upper levels of the atmosphere, caused by subsiding air from the Hadley cell, overlays moist, cool air rising from the surface. The strength of the trade wind inversion generally decreases from east to west.

Walker Circulation—A large-scale zonal (east-west) overturning of air in the tropical Pacific Ocean.

Weather—Instantaneous state of the atmosphere at any given time, mainly with respect to its effects on biological activities. As distinguished from climate, weather consists of the short-term (minutes to days) variations in the atmosphere. Popularly, weather is thought of in terms of temperature, precipitation, humidity, wind, sky condition, visibility, and cloud conditions.

Weather Element (same as climate element)—Attribute or property of the state of the atmosphere that is measured, estimated, or derived. Examples of weather elements include temperature, wind speed, wind direction, precipitation amount, precipitation type, relative humidity, dewpoint, solar radiation, snow depth, soil temperature at a given depth, etc. A derived weather element is a function of other elements (like degree days or number of days with rain) and is not measured directly. The terms "parameter" and "variable" are not used to describe weather elements.

Weather Network—Group of weather stations usually owned and maintained by a particular organization and usually for a specific purpose.

Weather Station—Station where collected data are intended for near-real-time use with less need for reference to long-term conditions. In many cases, the detailed circumstances of a set of measurements (siting and exposure, instrument changes, etc.) from weather stations are not as important as for climate stations.

Appendix C. Factors in operating a climate network.

C.1. Climate versus Weather
- Climate measurements require _consistency through time._

C.2. Network Purpose
- Anticipated or desired lifetime.
- Breadth of network mission (commitment by needed constituency).
- Dedicated constituency—no network survives without a dedicated constituency.

C.3. Site Identification and Selection
- Spanning gradients in climate or biomes with transects.
- Issues regarding representative spatial scale—site uniformity versus site clustering.
- Alignment with and contribution to network mission.
- Exposure—ability to measure representative quantities.
- Logistics—ability to service station (Always or only in favorable weather?).
- Site redundancy (positive for quality control, negative for extra resources).
- Power—is AC needed?
- Site security—is protection from vandalism needed?
- Permitting often a major impediment and usually underestimated.

C.4. Station Hardware
- Survival—weather is the main cause of lost weather/climate data.
- Robustness of sensors—ability to measure and record in any condition.
- Quality—distrusted records are worthless and a waste of time and money.
  - High quality—will cost up front but pays off later.
  - Low quality—may provide a lower start-up cost but will cost more later (low cost can be expensive).
- Redundancy—backup if sensors malfunction.
- Ice and snow—measurements are much more difficult than rain measurements.
- Severe environments (expense is about two–three times greater than for stations in more benign settings).

C.5. Communications
- Reliability—live data have a much larger constituency.
- One-way or two-way.
  - Retrieval of missed transmissions.
  - Ability to reprogram data logger remotely.
  - Remote troubleshooting abilities.
  - Continuing versus one-time costs.
- Back-up procedures to prevent data loss during communication outages.
- Live communications increase problems but also increase value.

C.6. Maintenance
- Main reason why networks fail (and most networks do eventually fail!).

- <u>Key</u> issue with nearly every network.
- Who will perform maintenance?
- Degree of commitment and motivation to contribute.
- Periodic? On-demand as needed? Preventive?
- Equipment change-out schedules and upgrades for sensors and software.
- Automated stations require <u>skilled</u> and <u>experienced</u> labor.
- Calibration—sensors often drift (climate).
- Site maintenance essential (constant vegetation, surface conditions, nearby influences).
- Typical automated station will cost about $2K per year to maintain.
- Documentation—photos, notes, visits, changes, essential for posterity.
- Planning for equipment life cycle and technological advances.

C.7. Maintaining Programmatic Continuity and Corporate Knowledge
- Long-term vision and commitment needed.
- Institutionalizing versus personalizing—developing appropriate dependencies.

C.8. Data Flow
- Centralized ingest?
- Centralized access to data and data products?
- Local version available?
- Contract out work or do it yourself?
- Quality control of data.
- Archival.
- Metadata—historic information, not a snapshot. Every station should collect metadata.
- Post-collection processing, multiple data-ingestion paths.

C.9. Products
- Most basic product consists of the data values.
- Summaries.
- Write own applications or leverage existing mechanisms?

C.10. Funding
- Prototype approaches as proof of concept.
- Linking and leveraging essential.
- Constituencies—every network <u>needs</u> a constituency.
- Bridging to practical and operational communities? Live data needed.
- Bridging to counterpart research efforts and initiatives—funding source.
- Creativity, resourcefulness, and persistence usually are essential to success.

C.11. Final Comments
- Deployment is by far the easiest part in operating a network.
- Maintenance is the main issue.
- Best analogy: Operating a network is like raising a child; it requires constant attention.

Source: Western Regional Climate Center (WRCC)

Appendix D. Master metadata field list.

Field Name	Field Type	Field Description
begin_date	date	Effective beginning date for a record.
begin_date_flag	char(2)	Flag describing the known accuracy of the begin date for a station.
best_elevation	float(4)	Best known elevation for a station (in feet).
clim_div_code	char(2)	Foreign key defining climate division code (primary in table: clim_div).
clim_div_key	int2	Foreign key defining climate division for a station (primary in table: clim_div.
clim_div_name	varchar(30)	English name for a climate division.
controller_info	varchar(50)	Person or organization who maintains the identifier system for a given weather or climate network.
country_key	int2	Foreign key defining country where a station resides (primary in table: none).
county_key	int2	Foreign key defining county where a station resides (primary in table: county).
county_name	varchar(31)	English name for a county.
description	text	Any description pertaining to the particular table.
end_date	date	Last effective date for a record.
end_date_flag	char(2)	Flag describing the known accuracy of station end date.
fips_country_code	char(2)	FIPS (federal information processing standards) country code.
fips_state_abbr	char(2)	FIPS state abbreviation for a station.
fips_state_code	char(2)	FIPS state code for a station.
history_flag	char(2)	Describes temporal significance of an individual record among others from the same station.
Id_type_key	int2	Foreign key defining the id_type for a station (usually defined in code).
last_updated	date	Date of last update for a record.
latitude	float(8)	Latitude value.
longitude	float(8)	Longitude value.
name_type_key	int2	"3": COOP station name, "2": best station name.
name	varchar(30)	Station name as known at date of last update entry.
ncdc_state_code	char(2)	NCDC, two-character code identifying U.S. state.
network_code	char(8)	Eight-character abbreviation code identifying a network.
network_key	int2	Foreign key defining the network for a station (primary in table: network).
network_station_id	int4	Identifier for a station in the associated network, which is defined by id_type_key.
remark	varchar(254)	Additional information for a record.
src_quality_code	char(2)	Code describing the data quality for the data source.
state_key	int2	Foreign key defining the U.S. state where a station resides (primary in table: state).
state_name	varchar(30)	English name for a state.
station_alt_name	varchar(30)	Other English names for a station.
station_best_name	varchar(30)	Best, most well-known English name for a station.
time_zone	float4	Time zone where a station resides.
ucan_station_id	int4	Unique station identifier for every station in ACIS.
unit_key	int2	Integer value representing a unit of measure.

Field Name	Field Type	Field Description
updated_by	char(8)	Person who last updated a record.
var_major_id	int2	Defines major climate variable.
var_minor_id	int2	Defines data source within a var_major_id.
zipcode	char(5)	Zipcode where a latitude/longitude point resides.
nps_netcode	char(4)	Network four-character identifier.
nps_netname	varchar(128)	Displayed English name for a network.
parkcode	char(4)	Park four-character identifier.
parkname	varchar(128)	Displayed English name for a park/
Im_network	char(4)	NPS I&M network where park belongs (a net code)/
station_id	varchar(16)	Station identifier.
station_id_type	varchar(16)	Type of station identifier.
network.subnetwork.id	varchar(16)	Identifier of a sub-network in associated network.
subnetwork_key	int2	Foreign key defining sub-network for a station.
subnetwork_name	varchar(30)	English name for a sub-network.
slope	integer	Terrain slope at the location.
aspect	integer	Terrain aspect at the station.
gps	char(1)	Indicator of latitude/longitude recorded via GPS (global positioning system).
site_description	text(0)	Physical description of site.
route_directions	text(0)	Driving route or site access directions.
station_photo_id	integer	Unique identifier associating a group of photos to a station. Group of photos all taken on same date.
photo_id	char(30)	Unique identifier for a photo.
photo_date	datetime	Date photograph taken.
photographer	varchar(64)	Name of photographer.
maintenance_date	datetime	Date of station maintenance visit.
contact_key	Integer	Unique identifier associating contact information to a station.
full_name	varchar(64)	Full name of contact person.
organization	varchar(64)	Organization of contact person.
contact_type	varchar(32)	Type of contact person (operator, administrator, etc.)
position_title	varchar(32)	Title of contact person.
address	varchar(32)	Address for contact person.
city	varchar(32)	City for contact person.
state	varchar(2)	State for contact person.
zip_code	char(10)	Zipcode for contact person.
country	varchar(32)	Country for contact person.
email	varchar(64)	E-mail for contact person.
work_phone	varchar(16)	Work phone for contact person.
contact_notes	text(254)	Other details regarding contact person.
equipment_type	char(30)	Sensor measurement type; i.e., wind speed, air temperature, etc.
eq_manufacturer	char(30)	Manufacturer of equipment.
eq_model	char(20)	Model number of equipment.
serial_num	char(20)	Serial number of equipment.
eq_description	varchar(254)	Description of equipment.
install_date	datetime	Installation date of equipment.
remove_date	datetime	Removal date of equipment.
ref_height	integer	Sensor displacement height from surface.
sampling_interval	varchar(10)	Frequency of sensor measurement.

Appendix E. General design considerations for weather/climate-monitoring programs.

The process for designing a climate-monitoring program benefits from anticipating design and protocol issues discussed here. Much of this material is been excerpted from a report addressing the Channel Islands National Park (Redmond and McCurdy 2005), where an example is found illustrating how these factors can be applied to a specific setting. Many national park units possess some climate or meteorology feature that sets them apart from more familiar or "standard" settings.

E.1. Introduction

There are several criteria that must be used in deciding to deploy new stations and where these new stations should be sited.

- Where are existing stations located?
- Where have data been gathered in the past (discontinued locations)?
- Where would a new station fill a knowledge gap about basic, long-term climatic averages for an area of interest?
- Where would a new station fill a knowledge gap about how climate behaves over time?
- As a special case for behavior over time, what locations might be expected to show a more sensitive response to climate change?
- How do answers to the preceding questions depend on the climate element? Are answers the same for precipitation, temperature, wind, humidity, etc.?
- What role should manual measurements play? How should manual measurements interface with automated measurements?
- Are there special technical or management issues, either present or anticipated in the next 5–15 years, requiring added climate information?
- What unique information is provided in addition to information from existing sites? "Redundancy is bad."
- What nearby information is available to estimate missing observations because observing systems always experience gaps and lose data? "Redundancy is good."
- How would logistics and maintenance affect these decisions?

In relation to the preceding questions, there are several topics that should be considered. The following topics are not listed in a particular order.

E.1.1. Network Purpose

Humans seem to have an almost reflexive need to measure temperature and precipitation, along with other climate elements. These reasons span a broad range from utilitarian to curiosity-driven. Although there are well-known recurrent patterns of need and data use, new uses are always appearing. The number of uses ranges in the thousands. Attempts have been made to categorize such uses (see NRC 1998; NRC 2001). Because climate measurements are accumulated over a long time, they should be treated as multi-purpose and should be undertaken in a manner that serves the widest possible applications. Some applications remain constant, while others rise and fall in importance. An insistent issue today may subside, while the next pressing issue of tomorrow barely may be anticipated. The notion that humans might affect the climate of the entire Earth was nearly unimaginable when the national USDA (later NOAA) cooperative weather network began in the late 1800s. Abundant experience has shown, however, that there always will be a demand for a history record of climate measurements and their properties. Experience also shows that there is an expectation that climate measurements will be taken and made available to the general public.

An exhaustive list of uses for data would fill many pages and still be incomplete. In broad terms, however, there are needs to document environmental conditions that disrupt or otherwise affect park operations (e.g., storms and droughts). Design and construction standards are determined by climatological event frequencies that exceed certain thresholds. Climate is a determinant that sometimes attracts and sometimes discourages visitors. Climate may play a large part in the park experience (e.g., Death Valley and heat are nearly synonymous). Some park units are large enough to encompass spatial or elevation diversity in climate, and the sequence of events can vary considerably inside or close to park boundaries. That is, temporal trends and statistics may not be the same everywhere, and this spatial structure should be sampled. The granularity of this structure depends on the presence of topography or large climate gradients or both, such as that found along the U.S. West Coast in summer with the rapid transition from the marine layer to the hot interior.

Plant and animal communities and entire ecosystems react to every nuance in the physical environment. No aspect of weather and climate goes undetected in the natural world. Wilson (1998) proposed "an informal rule of biological evolution" that applies here: "If an organic sensor can be imagined that is capable of detecting any particular environmental signal, a species exists somewhere that possesses this sensor." Every weather and climate event, whether dull or extraordinary to humans, matters to some organism. Dramatic events and creeping incremental change both have consequences to living systems. Extreme events or disturbances can "reset the clock" or "shake up the system" and lead to reverberations that last for years to centuries or longer. Slow change can carry complex nonlinear systems (e.g., any living assemblage) into states where chaotic transitions and new behavior occur. These changes are seldom predictable, typically are observed after the fact, and understood only in retrospect. Climate changes may not be exciting, but as a well-known atmospheric scientist, Mike Wallace, from the University of Washington once noted, "subtle does not mean unimportant".

Thus, individuals who observe the climate should be able to record observations accurately and depict both rapid and slow changes. In particular, an array of artificial influences easily can confound detection of slow changes. The record as provided can contain both real climate variability (that took place in the atmosphere) and fake climate variability (that arose directly from the way atmospheric changes were observed and recorded). As an example, trees growing near a climate station with an excellent anemometer will make it appear that the wind gradually slowed down over many years. Great care must be taken to protect against sources of fake climate variability on the longer-time scales of years to decades. Processes leading to the observed climate are not stationary; rather these processes draw from probability distributions that vary with time. For this reason, climatic time series do not exhibit statistical stationarity. The implications are manifold. There are no true climatic "normals" to which climate inevitably must return. Rather, there are broad ranges of climatic conditions. Climate does not demonstrate exact repetition but instead continual fluctuation and sometimes approximate repetition. In addition, there is always new behavior waiting to occur. Consequently, the business of climate monitoring is never finished, and there is no point where we can state confidently that "enough" is known.

E.1.2. Robustness

The most frequent cause for loss of weather data is the weather itself, the very thing we wish to record. The design of climate and weather observing programs should consider the meteorological equivalent of "peaking power" employed by utilities. Because environmental disturbances have significant effects on ecologic systems, sensors, data loggers, and communications networks should be able to function during the most severe conditions that realistically can be anticipated over the next 50–100 years. Systems designed in this manner are less likely to fail under more ordinary conditions, as well as more likely to transmit continuous, quality data for both tranquil and active periods.

E.1.3. Weather versus Climate

For "weather" measurements, pertaining to what is approximately happening here and now, small moves and changes in exposure are not as critical. For "climate" measurements, where values from different points in time are compared, siting and exposure are critical factors, and it is vitally important that the observing circumstances remain essentially unchanged over the duration of the station record.

Station moves can affect different elements to differing degrees. Even small moves of several meters, especially vertically, can affect temperature records. Hills and knolls act differently from the bottoms of small swales, pockets, or drainage channels (Whiteman 2000; Geiger et al. 2003). Precipitation is probably less subject to change with moves of 50–100 m than other elements (that is, precipitation has less intrinsic variation in small spaces) except if wind flow over the gauge is affected.

E.1.4. Physical Setting

Siting and exposure, and their continuity and consistency through time, significantly influence the climate records produced by a station. These two terms have overlapping connotations. We use the term "siting" in a more general sense, reserving the term "exposure" generally for the particular circumstances affecting the ability of an instrument to record measurements that are representative of the desired spatial or temporal scale.

E.1.5. Measurement Intervals

Climatic processes occur continuously in time, but our measurement systems usually record in discrete chunks of time: for example, seconds, hours, or days. These measurements often are referred to as "systematic" measurements. Interval averages may hide active or interesting periods of highly intense activity. Alternatively, some systems record "events" when a certain threshold of activity is exceeded (examples: another millimeter of precipitation has fallen, another kilometer of wind has moved past, the temperature has changed by a degree, a gust higher than 9.9 m/s has been measured). When this occurs, measurements from all sensors are reported. These measurements are known as "breakpoint" data. In relatively unchanging conditions (long calm periods or rainless weeks, for example), event recorders should send a signal that they are still "alive and well." If systematic recorders are programmed to note and periodically report the highest, lowest, and mean value within each time interval, the likelihood is reduced that interesting behavior will be glossed over or lost. With the capacity of modern data loggers, it is recommended to record and report extremes within the basic time increment (e.g., hourly or 10 minutes). This approach also assists quality-control procedures.

There is usually a trade-off between data volume and time increment, and most automated systems now are set to record approximately hourly. A number of field stations maintained by WRCC are programmed to record in 5- or 10-minute increments, which readily serve to construct an hourly value. However, this approach produces 6–12 times as much data as hourly data. These systems typically do not record details of events at sub-interval time scales, but they easily can record peak values, or counts of threshold exceedance, within the time intervals.

Thus, for each time interval at an automated station, we recommend that several kinds of information—mean or sum, extreme maximum and minimum, and sometimes standard deviation—be recorded. These measurements are useful for quality control and other purposes. Modern data loggers and office computers have quite high capacity. Diagnostic information indicating the state of solar chargers or battery voltages and their extremes is of great value. This topic will be discussed in greater detail in a succeeding section.

Automation also has made possible adaptive or intelligent monitoring techniques where systems vary the recording rate based on detection of the behavior of interest by the software. Sub-interval behavior of interest can be masked on occasion (e.g., a 5-minute extreme downpour with high-erosive capability hidden by an innocuous hourly total). Most users prefer measurements that are systematic in time because they are much easier to summarize and manipulate.

For breakpoint data produced by event reporters, there also is a need to send periodically a signal that the station is still functioning, even though there is nothing more to report. "No report" does not necessarily mean "no data," and it is important to distinguish between the actual observation that was recorded and the content of that observation (e.g., an observation of "0.00" is not the same as "no observation").

E.1.6. Mixed Time Scales

There are times when we may wish to combine information from radically different scales. For example, over the past 100 years we may want to know how the frequency of 5-minute precipitation peaks has varied or how the frequency of peak 1-second wind gusts have varied. We may also want to know over this time if nearby vegetation gradually has grown up to increasingly block the wind or to slowly improve precipitation catch. Answers to these questions require knowledge over a wide range of time scales.

E.1.7. Elements

For manual measurements, the typical elements recorded included temperature extremes, precipitation, and, in colder climates, snowfall/snow depth. Automated measurements typically include temperature, precipitation, humidity, wind speed and direction, and solar radiation. An exception to this exists in very windy locations where precipitation is difficult to measure accurately. Automated measurements of snow are improving, but manual measurements are still preferable, as long as shielding is present. Automated measurement of frozen precipitation presents numerous challenges that have not been resolved fully, and the best gauges are quite expensive ($3–8K). Soil temperatures also are included sometimes. Soil moisture is extremely useful, but measurements are not made at many sites. In addition, care must be taken in the installation and maintenance of instruments used in measuring soil moisture. Soil properties vary tremendously in short distances as well, and it is often very difficult ("impossible") to accurately document these variations (without digging up all the soil!). In cooler climates, ultrasonic sensors that detect snow depth are becoming commonplace.

E.1.8. Wind Standards

Wind varies the most in the shortest distance, since it always decreases to zero near the ground and increases rapidly (approximately logarithmically) with height near the ground. Changes in anemometer height obviously will affect distribution of wind speed as will changes in vegetation, obstructions such as buildings, etc. A site that has a 3-m (10-ft) mast clearly will be less windy than a site that has a 6-m (20-ft) or 10-m (33-ft) mast. Historically, many U.S. airports (FAA and NWS) and most current RAWS sites have used a standard 6-m (20-ft) mast for wind measurements. Some NPS RAWS sites utilize shorter masts. Over the last decade, as Automated Surface Observing Systems (ASOSs, mostly NWS) and Automated Weather Observing Systems (AWOSs, mostly FAA) have been deployed at most airports, wind masts have been raised to 8 or 10 m (26 or 33 ft), depending on airplane clearance. The World Meteorological Organization recommends 10 m as the height for wind measurements (WMO 1983; 2005), and more groups are migrating slowly to this standard. The American Association of State Climatologists (AASC 1985) have recommended that wind be measured at 3 m, a standard geared more for agricultural applications than for general purpose uses where higher levels usually are preferred. Different anemometers have different starting thresholds; therefore, areas that frequently experience very light winds may not produce wind measurements thus affecting long-term mean estimates of wind speed. For both sustained winds (averages over a short interval of 2–60 minutes) and especially for gusts, the duration of the sampling interval makes considerable difference. For the same wind history, 1–second gusts are higher than gusts averaging 3 seconds, which in turn are greater than 5-second averages, so that the same sequence would be described with different numbers (all three systems and more are in use). Changes in the averaging procedure, or in height or exposure, can lead to "false" or "fake" climate change with no change in actual climate. Changes in any of these should be noted in the metadata.

E.1.9. Wind Nomenclature

Wind is a vector quantity having a direction and a speed. Directions can be two- or three-dimensional; they will be three-dimensional if the vertical component is important. In all common uses, winds always are denoted by the direction they blow *from* (north wind or southerly breeze). This convention exists because wind often brings weather, and thus our attention is focused upstream. However, this approach contrasts with the way ocean currents are viewed. Ocean currents usually are denoted by the direction they are moving *towards* (e.g., an eastward current moves from west to east). In specialized applications (such as in atmospheric modeling), wind velocity vectors point in the direction that the wind is blowing. Thus, a southwesterly wind (from the southwest) has both northward and eastward (to the north and to the east) components. Except near mountains, wind cannot blow up or down near the ground, so the vertical component of wind often is approximated as zero, and the horizontal component is emphasized.

E.1.10. Frozen Precipitation

Frozen precipitation is more difficult to measure than liquid precipitation, especially with automated techniques. Goodison et al. (1998), Sevruk and Harmon (1984), Yang et al. (1998; 2001) provide many of the reasons to explain this. The importance of frozen precipitation varies greatly from one setting to another. This subject was discussed in greater detail in a related inventory and monitoring report for the Alaska park units (Redmond et al. 2005).

In climates that receive frozen precipitation, a decision must be made whether or not to try to record such events accurately. This usually means that the precipitation must be turned into liquid either by falling into an antifreeze fluid solution that is then weighed or by heating the precipitation enough to melt and fall through a measuring mechanism such as a nearly-balanced tipping bucket. Accurate measurements from the first approach require expensive gauges; tipping buckets can achieve this resolution readily but are more apt to lose some or all precipitation. Improvements have been made to the heating mechanism on the NWS tipping-bucket gauge used for the ASOS to correct its numerous deficiencies making it less problematic; however, this gauge is not inexpensive. A heat supply needed to melt frozen precipitation usually requires more energy than renewable energy (solar panels or wind recharging) can provide thus AC power is needed.

E.1.11. Save or Lose

A second consideration with precipitation is determining if the measurement should be saved (as in weighing systems) or lost (as in tipping-bucket systems). With tipping buckets, after the water has passed through the tipping mechanism, it usually just drops to the ground. Thus, there is no checksum to ensure that the sum of all the tips adds up to what has been saved in a reservoir at some location. By contrast, the weighing gauges continually accumulate until the reservoir is emptied, the reported value is the total reservoir content (for example, the height of the liquid column in a tube), and the incremental precipitation is the difference in depth between two known times. These weighing gauges do not always have the same fine resolution. Some gauges only record to the nearest centimeter, which is usually acceptable for hydrology but not necessarily for other needs. (For reference, a millimeter of precipitation can get a person in street clothes quite wet.)

E.1.12. Time

Time should always be in local standard time (LST), and daylight savings time (DST) should never be used under any circumstances with automated equipment and timers. Using DST leads to one duplicate hour, one missing hour, and a season of displaced values, as well as needless confusion and a data-management nightmare. Absolute time, such as Greenwich Mean Time (GMT) or Coordinated Universal Time (UTC), also can be used because these formats are unambiguously translatable. Since measurements only provide information about what already *has* occurred or *is* occurring and not what *will* occur, they should always be assigned to the *ending time* of the associated interval with hour 24 marking the end of the last hour of the day. In this system, midnight always represents the end of the day, not the start. To demonstrate the importance of this differentiation, we have encountered situations where police officers seeking corroborating weather data could not recall whether the time on their crime report from a year ago was the starting midnight or the ending midnight! Station positions should be known to within a few meters, easily accomplished with GPS, so that time zones and solar angles can be determined accurately.

E.1.13. Automated versus Manual

Most of this report has addressed automated measurements. Historically, most measurements are manual and typically collected once a day. In many cases, manual measurements continue because of habit, usefulness, and desire for continuity over time. Manual measurements are extremely useful and when possible should be encouraged. However, automated measurements are becoming more common. For either, it is important to record time in a logically consistent manner.

It should not be automatically assumed that newer data and measurements are "better" than older data or that manual data are "worse" than automated data. Older or simpler manual measurements are often of very high quality even if they sometimes are not in the most convenient digital format.

There is widespread desire to use automated systems to reduce human involvement. This is admirable and understandable, but every automated weather/climate station or network requires significant human attention and maintenance. A telling example concerns the Oklahoma Mesonet (see Brock et al. 1995, and bibliography at http://www.mesonet.ou.edu), a network of about 115 high–quality, automated meteorological stations spread over Oklahoma, where about 80 percent of the annual ($2–3M) budget is nonetheless allocated to humans with only about 20 percent allocated to equipment.

E.1.14. Manual Conventions

Manual measurements typically are made once a day. Elements usually consist of maximum and minimum temperature, temperature at observation time, precipitation, snowfall, snow depth, and sometimes evaporation, wind, or other information. Since it is not actually known when extremes occurred, the only logical approach, and the nationwide convention, is to ascribe the entire measurement to the time-interval date and to enter it on the form in that way. For morning observers (for example, 8 am to 8 am), this means that the maximum temperature written for today often is from yesterday afternoon and sometimes the minimum temperature for the 24-hr period actually occurred yesterday morning. However, this is understood and expected. It is often a surprise to observers to see how many maximum temperatures do not occur in the afternoon and how many minimum temperatures do not occur in the predawn hours. This is especially true in environments that are colder, higher, northerly, cloudy, mountainous, or coastal. As long as this convention is strictly followed every day, it has been shown that truly excellent climate records can result (Redmond 1992). Manual observers should reset equipment only one time per day at the official observing time. Making more than one measurement a day is discouraged strongly; this practice results in a hybrid record that is too difficult to interpret. The only exception is for total daily snowfall. New snowfall can be measured up to four times per day with no observations closer than six hours. It is well known that more frequent measurement of snow increases the annual total because compaction is a continuous process.

Two main purposes for climate observations are to establish the long-term averages for given locations and to track variations in climate. Broadly speaking, these purposes address topics of absolute and relative climate behavior. Once absolute behavior has been "established" (a task that is never finished because long-term averages continue to vary in time)—temporal variability quickly becomes the item of most interest.

E.2. Representativeness

Having discussed important factors to consider when new sites are installed, we now turn our attention to site "representativeness." In popular usage, we often encounter the notion that a site is "representative" of another site if it receives the same annual precipitation or records the same annual temperature or if some other element-specific, long-term average has a similar value. This notion of representativeness has a certain limited validity, but there are other aspects of this idea that need to be considered.

A climate monitoring site also can be said to be representative if climate records from that site show sufficiently strong temporal correlations with a large number of locations over a sufficiently large area. If station A receives 20 cm a year and station B receives 200 cm a year, these climates obviously receive quite differing amounts of precipitation. However, if their monthly, seasonal, or annual correlations are high (for example, 0.80 or higher for a particular time scale), one site can be used as a surrogate for estimating values at the other if measurements for a particular month, season, or year are missing. That is, a wet or dry month at one station is also a wet or dry month (relative to its own mean) at the comparison station. Note that high correlations on one time scale do not imply automatically that high correlations will occur on other time scales.

Likewise, two stations having similar mean climates (for example, similar annual precipitation) might not co-vary in close synchrony (for example, coastal versus interior). This may be considered a matter of climate "affiliation" for a particular location.

Thus, the representativeness of a site can refer either to the basic climatic averages for a given duration (or time window within the annual cycle) or to the extent that the site co-varies in time with respect to all surrounding locations. One site can be representative of another in the first sense but not the second, or vice versa, or neither, or both—all combinations are possible.

If two sites are perfectly correlated then, in a sense, they are "redundant." However, redundancy has value because all sites will experience missing data especially with automated equipment in rugged environments and harsh climates where outages and other problems nearly can be guaranteed. In many cases, those outages are caused by the weather, particularly by unusual weather and the very conditions we most wish to know about. Methods for filling in those values will require proxy information from this or other nearby networks. Thus, redundancy is a virtue rather than a vice.

In general, the cooperative stations managed by the NWS have produced much longer records than automated stations like RAWS stations. The RAWS stations often have problems with precipitation, especially in winter, or with missing data, so that low correlations may be data problems rather than climatic dissimilarity. The RAWS records also are relatively short, so correlations should be interpreted with care. In performing and interpreting such analyses, however, we must remember that there are physical climate reasons and observational reasons why stations within a short distance (even a few tens or hundreds of meters) may not correlate well.

E.2.1. Temporal Behavior

It is possible that high correlations will occur between station pairs during certain portions of the year (i.e., January) but low correlations may occur during other portions of the year (e.g., September or October). The relative contributions of these seasons to the annual total (for precipitation) or average (for temperature) and the correlations for each month are both factors in the correlation of an aggregated time window of longer duration that encompasses those seasons (e.g., one of the year definitions such as calendar year or water year). A complete and careful evaluation ideally would include such a correlation analysis but requires more resources and data. Note that it also is possible and frequently is observed that temperatures are highly correlated while precipitation is not or vice versa, and these relations can change according to the time of year. If two stations are well correlated for all climate elements for all portions of the year, then they can be considered redundant.

With scarce resources, the initial strategy should be to try to identify locations that do not correlate particularly well, so that each new site measures something new that cannot be guessed easily from the behavior of surrounding sites. (An important caveat here is that lack of such correlation could be a result of physical climate behavior and not a result of faults with the actual measuring process; i.e., by unrepresentative or simply poor-quality data. Unfortunately, we seldom have perfect climate data.) As additional sites are added, we usually wish for some combination of unique and redundant sites to meet what amounts to essentially orthogonal constraints: new information and more reliably-furnished information.

Unfortunately, we do not have stations everywhere, so we are forced to use the few comparisons that we have and include a large dose of intelligent reasoning, using what we have observed elsewhere. In performing and interpreting such analyses, we must remember that there are physical climatic reasons and observational reasons why stations within a short distance (even a few tens or hundreds of meters) may not correlate well.

Examples of correlation analyses include those for the Channel Islands and for southwest Alaska, which can be found in Redmond and McCurdy (2005) and Redmond et al. (2005). These examples illustrate what can be learned from correlation analyses. Spatial correlations generally vary by time of year. Thus, results should be displayed in the form of annual correlation cycles—for monthly mean temperature and monthly total precipitation and perhaps other climate elements like wind or humidity—between station pairs selected for climatic setting and data availability and quality.

In general, the COOP stations managed by the NWS have produced much longer records than have automated stations like RAWS stations. The RAWS stations also often have problems with precipitation, especially in winter or with missing data, so that low correlations may be data problems rather than climate dissimilarity. The RAWS records are much shorter, so correlations should be interpreted with care, but these stations are more likely to be in places of interest for remote or under-sampled regions.

E.2.2. Spatial Behavior

A number of techniques exist to interpolate from isolated point values to a spatial domain. For example, a common technique is simple inverse distance weighting. Critical to the success of the simplest of such techniques is that some other property of the spatial domain, one that is influential for the mapped element, does not vary significantly. Topography greatly influences precipitation, temperature, wind, humidity, and most other meteorological elements. Thus, this criterion clearly is not met in any region having extreme topographic diversity. In such circumstances, simple Cartesian distance may have little to do with how rapidly correlation deteriorates from one site to the next, and in fact, the correlations can decrease readily from a mountain to a valley and then increase again on the next mountain. Such structure in the fields of spatial correlation is not seen in the relatively (statistically) well-behaved flat areas like those in the eastern U.S.

To account for dominating effects such as topography and inland–coastal differences that exist in certain regions, some kind of additional knowledge must be brought to bear to produce meaningful, physically plausible, and observationally based interpolations. Historically, this has proven to be an extremely difficult problem, especially to perform objective and repeatable analyses. An analysis performed for southwest Alaska (Redmond et al. 2005) concluded that the PRISM (Parameter Regression on Independent Slopes Model) maps (Daly et al. 1994; 2002; Gibson et al. 2002; Doggett et al. 2004) were probably the best available. An analysis by Simpson et al. (2005) further discussed many issues in the mapping of Alaska's climate and resulted in the same conclusion about PRISM.

E.2.3. Climate-Change Detection

Although general purpose climate stations should be situated to address all aspects of climate variability, it is desirable that they also be in locations that are more sensitive to climate change from natural or anthropogenic influences should it begin to occur. The question here is how well we know such sensitivities. The climate-change issue is quite complex because it encompasses more than just greenhouse gasses.

Sites that are in locations or climates particularly vulnerable to climate change should be favored. How this vulnerability is determined is a considerably challenging research issue. Candidate locations or situations are those that lie on the border between two major biomes or just inside the edge of one or the other. In these cases, a slight movement of the boundary in anticipated direction (toward "warmer," for example) would be much easier to detect as the boundary moves past the site and a different set of biota begin to be established. Such a vegetative or ecologic response would be more visible and would take less time to establish as a real change than would a smaller change in the center of the distribution range of a marker or key species.

E.2.4. Element-Specific Differences

The various climate elements (temperature, precipitation, cloudiness, snowfall, humidity, wind speed and direction, solar radiation) do not vary through time in the same sequence or manner nor should they necessarily be expected to vary in this manner. The spatial patterns of variability should not be expected to be the same for all elements. These patterns also should not be expected to be similar for all months or seasons. The suitability of individual sites for measurement also varies from one element to another. A site that has a favorable exposure for temperature or wind may not have a favorable exposure for precipitation. A site that experiences proper air movement may be situated in a topographic channel, such as a river valley, which restricts the range of wind directions and affects the distribution of speed-direction categories.

E.2.5. Logistics and Practical Factors

Even with the most advanced scientific rationale, sites in some remote or climatically challenging settings may not be suitable because of the difficulty in servicing and maintaining equipment. Contributing to these challenges are scheduling difficulties, access and logistical problems, and the weather itself. Remote and elevated sites usually require far more attention and expense than an easily-accessible valley location.

For climate purposes, station exposure and the local environment should be maintained in their original state (vegetation especially), so that changes seen are the result of regional climate variations and not of trees growing up, bushes crowding a site, surface albedo changing, fire clearing, etc. Repeat photography has shown many examples of slow environmental change in the vicinity of a station in rather short time frames (5–20 years), and this technique should be employed routinely and frequently at all locations. In the end, logistics, maintenance, and other practical factors almost always determine the success of weather- and climate-monitoring activities.

E.2.6. Personnel Factors

Many past experiences (almost exclusively negative) strongly support the necessity to place primary responsibility for station deployment and maintenance in the hands of seasoned, highly qualified, trained, and meticulously careful personnel, the more experienced the better. Over time, even in "benign" climates but especially where harsher conditions prevail, every conceivable problem will occur and both the usual and unusual should be anticipated: weather, animals, plants, salt, sensor and communication failure, windblown debris, corrosion, power failures, vibrations, flash floods, landslides, fires,corruption of the data logger program, etc. An ability to anticipate and forestall such problems, a knack for innovation and improvisation, knowledge of electronics, practical and organizational skills, and presence of mind to bring the various small but vital parts, spares, tools, and diagnostic troubleshooting equipment are highly valued qualities. Especially when logistics are so expensive, a premium should be placed on using experienced personnel, since the slightest and seemingly most minor mistake can render a station useless or, even worse, uncertain. Exclusive reliance on individuals without this background can be costly and almost always will result eventually in unnecessary loss of data. Skilled labor and an apprenticeship system to develop new skilled labor will greatly reduce (but not eliminate) the types of problems that can occur in operating a climate network.

E.3. Site Selection

In addition to considerations identified previously in this appendix, various factors need to be considered in selecting sites for new or augmented instrumentation.

E.3.1. Equipment and Exposure Factors

E.3.1.1. Measurement Suite: All sites should measure temperature, humidity, wind, solar radiation, and, in colder climates, snow depth. Precipitation measurements are more difficult but probably should be attempted with the understanding that winter measurements may be of limited or no value unless an all-weather gauge has been installed. Even if an all-weather gauge has been installed, it is desirable to have a second gauge present that operates on a different principle–for example, a fluid-based system in tandem with a higher–resolution, tipping bucket gauge for summertime.

E.3.1.2. Overall Exposure: The ideal, general all-purpose site has gentle slopes, is open to the sun and the wind, has a natural vegetative cover, avoids strong local (less than 200 m) influences, and represents a reasonable compromise among all climate elements. The best temperature sites are not the best precipitation sites, and the same is true for other elements. Steep topography in the immediate vicinity should be avoided unless settings where precipitation is affected by steep topography are being deliberately sought or a mountaintop or ridgeline is the desired location. The potential for disturbance should be considered: fire and flood risk, earth movement, wind-borne debris, volcanic deposits or lahars, vandalism, animal tampering, and general human encroachment are all factors.

E.3.1.3. Elevation: Higher-elevation climates do not vary in time in exactly the same manner as adjoining low-elevation climates. This concept is emphasized when temperature inversions are present to a greater degree and during precipitation when winds rise up the slopes at the same angle. There is considerable concern that mountain climates will be (or already are) changing and perhaps changing differently than lowland climates, which has direct and indirect consequences for plant and animal life in the more extreme zones. Elevations of special significance are those that are near the mean rain/snow line for winter, near the tree line, and near the mean annual freezing level (all of these may not be quite the same). Because the lapse rates in wet climates often are nearly moist-adiabatic during the main precipitation seasons, measurements at one elevation may be extrapolated to nearby elevations. In drier climates and in the winter, temperature and to a lesser extent wind will show various elevation profiles.

E.3.1.4. Transects: The concept of observing transects that span climatic gradients is sound. This is not always straightforward in topographically uneven terrain, but these transects could still be arranged by setting up station(s) along the coast; in or near passes atop the main coastal interior drainage divide; and inland at one, two, or three distances into the interior lowlands. Transects need not—and by dint of topographic constraints probably cannot—be straight lines, but the closer that a line can be approximated the better. The main point is to systematically sample the key points of a behavioral transition without deviating too radically from linearity.

E.3.1.5. Other Topographic Considerations: There are various considerations with respect to local topography. Local topography can influence wind (channeling, upslope/downslope, etc.), precipitation (orographic enhancement, downslope evaporation, catch efficiency, etc.), and temperature (valleys, hilltops, aspect, mixing or decoupling from the overlying atmosphere, bowls, radiative effects, etc.), to different degrees at differing scales. In general, for measurements to be areally representative, it is better to avoid these local effects to the extent that they can be identified before station deployment (once deployed, it is desirable not to move a station). The primary purpose of a climate-monitoring network should be to serve as an infrastructure in the form of a set of benchmark stations for comparing other stations. Sometimes, however, it is exactly these local phenomena that we want to capture. Living organisms, especially plants, are affected by their immediate environment, whether it is representative of a larger setting or not. Specific measurements of limited scope and duration made for these purposes then can be tied to the main benchmarks. This experience is useful also in determining the complexity needed in the benchmark monitoring process in order to capture particular phenomena at particular space and time scales.

Sites that drain (cooler air) well generally are better than sites that allow cooler air to pool. Slightly sloped areas (1 degree is fine) or small benches from tens to hundreds of meters above streams are often favorable locations. Furthermore, these sites often tend to be out of the path of hazards (like floods) and to have rocky outcroppings where controlling vegetation will not be a major concern. Benches or wide spots on the rise between two forks of a river system are often the only flat areas and sometimes jut out to give greater exposure to winds from more directions.

E.3.1.6. Prior History: The starting point in designing a program is to determine what kinds of observations have been collected over time, by whom, in what manner, and if these observation are continuing to the present time. It also may be of value to "re-occupy" the former site of a station that is now inactive to provide some measure of continuity or a reference point from the past. This can be of value even if continuous observations were not made during the entire intervening period.

E.3.2. Element-Specific Factors

E.3.2.1. Temperature: An open exposure with uninhibited air movement is the preferred setting. The most common measurement is made at approximately eye level, 1.5–2.0 m. Sensors should be shielded above and below from solar radiation (bouncing off snow), from sunrise/sunset horizontal input, and from vertical rock faces. Sensors should be clamped tightly, so that they do not swivel away from level stacks of radiation plates. Nearby vegetation should be kept away from the sensors (several meters). Growing vegetation should be cut to original conditions. Small hollows and swales can cool tremendously at night, and it is best avoid these areas. Side slopes of perhaps a degree or two of angle facilitate air movement and drainage and, in effect, sample a large area during nighttime hours. The very bottom of a valley should be avoided. Temperature can change substantially from moves of only a few meters. Situations have been observed where flat and seemingly uniform conditions (like airport runways) appear to demonstrate different climate behaviors over short distances of a few tens or hundreds of meters (differences of 5–10°C).

E.3.2.2. Precipitation (liquid): Calm locations with vegetative or artificial shielding are preferred. Wind will adversely impact readings; therefore, the less the better. Wind effects on precipitation are far less for rain than for snow. Devices that "save" precipitation present advantages, but most gauges are built to dump precipitation as it falls or to empty periodically. Automated gauges give both the amount and the timing. Simple backups that record only the total precipitation since the last visit have a certain advantage (for example, storage gauges or lengths of PVC pipe perhaps with bladders on the bottom). The following question should be asked: Does the total precipitation from an automated gauge add up to the measured total in a simple bucket (evaporation is prevented with an appropriate substance such as mineral oil)? Drip from overhanging foliage and trees can augment precipitation totals.

E.3.2.3. Precipitation (frozen): Calm locations or shielding are a must. Undercatch for rain is only about 5 percent, but with winds of only 2–4 m/s, gauges may catch only 30–70 percent of the actual snow falling depending on density of the flakes. To catch 100 percent of the snow, the standard configuration for shielding is employed by the CRN (Climate Reference Network): the DFIR (Double-Fence Intercomparison Reference) shield with 2.4-m (8-ft.) vertical, wooden slatted fences in two concentric octagons with diameters of 8 m and 4 m (26 ft and 13 ft, respectively) and an inner Alter shield (flapping vanes). Numerous tests have shown this is the only way to achieve complete catch of snowfall (e.g., Yang et al. 1998; 2001). The DFIR shield is large and bulky; it is recommended that all precipitation gauges have at least Alter shields on them.

Artificial shielding (vanes, etc.) placed around gauges in locations that receive snow always should be used if accurate totals are desired. Moving parts tend to freeze up. Capping of gauges during heavy snowfall events is a common occurrence. When the cap becomes pointed, snow falls off to the ground and is not recorded. Caps and plugs often will not fall into the tube until hours, days, or even weeks have passed, typically during an extended period of freezing temperature or above or when sunlight finally occurs. Liquid-based measurements do not have the resolution (usually 0.3 cm [0.1 in.] rather than 0.03 cm [0.01 in.]) that tipping bucket and other gauges have but are known to be reasonably accurate. Light snowfall events might not be recorded until enough of them add up to the next reporting increment. More expensive gauges like Geonors can be considered; however, they need to be emptied every 40 cm (15 in.) or so (capacity of 51 cm [20 in.]) until the new 91-cm (36-in.) capacity gauge is offered for sale. Recently, the NWS has been trying out the new (and very expensive) Ott all-weather gauge. Riming can be an issue in windy foggy environments below freezing. Rime, dew, and other forms of atmospheric condensation are not real precipitation, since they are caused by the gauge.

E.3.2.4. Snow Depth: Windswept areas tend to be blown clear of snow. Conversely, certain types of vegetation can act as a snow fence and cause artificial drifts. However, some amount of vegetation in the vicinity generally can help slow down the wind. The two most common types of snow-depth gauges are the Judd Snow Depth Sensor, produced by Judd Communications, and the snow depth gauge produced by Campbell Scientific, Inc. Opinions vary on which one is better. These gauges use ultrasound and look downward in a cone about 22 degrees in diameter. The ground should be relatively clear of vegetation and maintained in a manner so that the zero point on the calibration scale does not change.

E.3.2.5. Snow Water Equivalent: This is determined by the weight of snow on fluid-filled pads about the size of a desktop set up sometimes in groups of four or in larger hexagons several meters in diameter. These pads require flat ground some distance from nearby sources of windblown snow and shielding that is "just right": not too close to the shielding to act as a kind of snow fence and not too far from the shielding so that blowing and drifting become a factor. Generally, these pads require fluids that possess antifreeze-like properties, as well as handling and replacement protocols.

E.3.2.6. Wind: Open exposures are needed for wind measurements. Small prominences or benches without blockage from certain sectors are preferred. A typical rule for trees is to site stations back 10 tree-heights from all tree obstructions. Sites in long, narrow valleys can obviously only exhibit two main wind directions. Gently rounded eminences are more favored. Any kind of topographic steering should be avoided to the extent possible. Avoiding major mountain chains or single isolated mountains or ridges is usually a favorable approach, if there is a choice. Sustained wind speed and the highest gusts (1-second) should be recorded. Averaging methodologies for both sustained winds and gusts can affect climate trends and should be recorded as metadata with all changes noted. Vegetation growth affects the vertical wind profile, and growth over a few years can lead to changes in mean wind speed even if the "real" wind does not change, so vegetation near the site (perhaps out to 50 m) should be maintained in a quasi-permanent status (same height and spatial distribution). Wind devices can rime up and freeze or spin out of balance. In severely rimed or windy climates, rugged anemometers, such as those made by Taylor, are worth considering. These anemometers are expensive but durable and can withstand substantial abuse. In exposed locations, personnel should plan for winds to be at least 50 m/s and be able to measure these wind speeds. At a minimum, anemometers should be rated to 75 m/s.

E.3.2.7. Humidity: Humidity is a relatively straightforward climate element. Close proximity to lakes or other water features can affect readings. Humidity readings typically are less accurate near 100 percent and at low humidities in cold weather.

E.3.2.8. Solar Radiation: A site with an unobstructed horizon obviously is the most desirable. This generally implies a flat plateau or summit. However, in most locations trees or mountains will obstruct the sun for part of the day.

E.3.2.9. Soil Temperature: It is desirable to measure soil temperature at locations where soil is present. If soil temperature is recorded at only a single depth, the most preferred depth is 10 cm. Other common depths include 25 cm, 50 cm, 2 cm, and 100 cm. Biological activity in the soil will be proportional to temperature with important threshold effects occurring near freezing.

E.3.2.10. Soil Moisture: Soil moisture gauges are somewhat temperamental and require care to install. The soil should be characterized by a soil expert during installation of the gauge. The readings may require a certain level of experience to interpret correctly. If accurate, readings of soil moisture are especially useful.

E.3.2.11. Distributed Observations: It can be seen readily that compromises must be struck among the considerations described in the preceding paragraphs because some are mutually exclusive.

How large can a "site" be? Generally, the equipment footprint should be kept as small as practical with all components placed next to each other (within less than 10–20 m or so). Readings from one instrument frequently are used to aid in interpreting readings from the remaining instruments.

What is a tolerable degree of separation? Some consideration may be given to locating a precipitation gauge or snow pillow among protective vegetation, while the associated temperature, wind, and humidity readings would be collected more effectively in an open and exposed location within 20–50 m. Ideally, it is advantageous to know the wind measurement precisely at the precipitation gauge, but a compromise involving a short split, and in effect a "distributed observation," could be considered. There are no definitive rules governing this decision, but it is suggested that the site footprint be kept within approximately 50 m. There also are constraints imposed by engineering and electrical factors that affect cable lengths, signal strength, and line noise; therefore, the shorter the cable the better. Practical issues include the need to trench a channel to outlying instruments or to allow lines to lie atop the ground and associated problems with animals, humans, weathering, etc. Separating a precipitation gauge up to 100 m or so from an instrument mast may be an acceptable compromise if other factors are not limiting.

E.3.2.12. Instrument Replacement Schedules: Instruments slowly degrade, and a plan for replacing them with new, refurbished, or recalibrated instruments should be in place. After approximately five years, a systematic change-out procedure should result in replacing most sensors in a network. Certain parts, such as solar radiation sensors, are candidates for annual calibration or change-out. Anemometers tend to degrade as bearings erode or electrical contacts become uneven. Noisy bearings are an indication, and a stethoscope might aid in hearing such noises. Increased internal friction affects the threshold starting speed; once spinning, they tend to function properly. Increases in starting threshold speeds can lead to more zero-wind measurements and thus reduce the reported mean wind speed with no real change in wind properties. A field calibration kit should be developed and taken on all site visits, routine or otherwise. Rain gauges can be tested with drip testers during field visits. Protective conduit and tight water seals can prevent abrasion and moisture problems with the equipment, although seals can keep moisture in as well as out. Bulletproof casings sometimes are employed in remote settings. A supply of spare parts, at least one of each and more for less-expensive or more-delicate sensors, should be maintained to allow replacement of worn or nonfunctional instruments during field visits. In addition, this approach allows instruments to be calibrated in the relative convenience of the operational home—the larger the network, the greater the need for a parts depot.

E.3.3. Long-Term Comparability and Consistency

E.3.3.1. Consistency: The emphasis here is to hold biases constant. Every site has biases, problems, and idiosyncrasies of one sort or another. The best rule to follow is simply to try to keep biases constant through time. Since the goal is to track climate through time, keeping sensors, methodologies, and exposure constant will ensure that only true climate change is being measured. This means leaving the site in its original state or performing maintenance to keep it that way. Once a site is installed, the goal should be to never move the site even by a few meters or to allow significant changes to occur within 100 m for the next several decades.

Sites in or near rock outcroppings likely will experience less vegetative disturbance or growth through the years and will not usually retain moisture, a factor that could speed corrosion. Sites that will remain locally similar for some time are usually preferable. However, in some cases the intent of a station might be to record the local climate effects of changes within a small-scale system (for example, glacier, recently burned area, or scene of some other disturbance) that is subject to a regional climate influence. In this example, the local changes might be much larger than the regional changes.

E.3.3.2. Metadata: Since the climate of every site is affected by features in the immediate vicinity, it is vital to record this information over time and to update the record repeatedly at each service visit. Distances, angles, heights of vegetation, fine-scale topography, condition of instruments, shielding discoloration, and other factors from within a meter to several kilometers should be noted. Systematic photography should be undertaken and updated at least once every one–two years.

Photographic documentation should be taken at each site in a standard manner and repeated every two–three years. Guidelines for methodology were developed by Redmond (2004) as a result of experience with the NOAA CRN and can be found on the WRCC NPS Web pages at www.wrcc.dri.edu/nps and at ftp.wrcc.dri.edu/nps/photodocumentation.pdf.

The main purpose for climate stations is to *track climatic conditions through time*. Anything that affects the interpretation of records through time must to be noted and recorded for posterity. The important factors should be clear to a person who has never visited the site, no matter how long ago the site was installed.

In regions with significant, climatic transition zones, transects are an efficient way to span several climates and make use of available resources. Discussions on this topic at greater detail can be found in Redmond and Simeral (2004) and in Redmond et al. (2005).

E.4. Literature Cited

American Association of State Climatologists. 1985. Heights and exposure standards for sensors on automated weather stations. The State Climatologist **9**.

Brock, F. V., K. C. Crawford, R. L. Elliott, G. W. Cuperus, S. J. Stadler, H. L. Johnson and M. D. Eilts. 1995. The Oklahoma Mesonet: A technical overview. Journal of Atmospheric and Oceanic Technology **12**:5-19.

Daly, C., R. P. Neilson, and D. L. Phillips. 1994. A statistical-topographic model for mapping climatological precipitation over mountainous terrain. Journal of Applied Meteorology **33**:140-158.

Daly, C., W. P. Gibson, G. H. Taylor, G. L. Johnson, and P. Pasteris. 2002. A knowledge-based approach to the statistical mapping of climate. Climate Research **22**:99-113.

Doggett, M., C. Daly, J. Smith, W. Gibson, G. Taylor, G. Johnson, and P. Pasteris. 2004. High-resolution 1971-2000 mean monthly temperature maps for the western United States. Fourteenth AMS Conf. on Applied Climatology, 84th AMS Annual Meeting. Seattle, WA, American Meteorological Society, Boston, MA, January 2004, Paper 4.3, CD-ROM.

Geiger, R., R. H. Aron, and P. E. Todhunter. 2003. The Climate Near the Ground. 6th edition. Rowman & Littlefield Publishers, Inc., New York.

Gibson, W. P., C. Daly, T. Kittel, D. Nychka, C. Johns, N. Rosenbloom, A. McNab, and G. Taylor. 2002. Development of a 103-year high-resolution climate data set for the conterminous United States. Thirteenth AMS Conf. on Applied Climatology. Portland, OR, American Meteorological Society, Boston, MA, May 2002:181-183.

Goodison, B. E., P. Y. T. Louie, and D. Yang. 1998. WMO solid precipitation measurement intercomparison final report. WMO TD 982, World Meteorological Organization, Geneva, Switzerland.

National Research Council. 1998. Future of the National Weather Service Cooperative Weather Network. National Academies Press, Washington, D.C.

National Research Council. 2001. A Climate Services Vision: First Steps Toward the Future. National Academies Press, Washington, D.C.

Redmond, K. T. 1992. Effects of observation time on interpretation of climatic time series - A need for consistency. Eighth Annual Pacific Climate (PACLIM) Workshop. Pacific Grove, CA, March 1991:141-150.

Redmond, K. T. 2004. Photographic documentation of long-term climate stations. Available from ftp://ftp.wrcc.dri.edu/nps/photodocumentation.pdf. (accessed 15 August 2004)

Redmond, K. T. and D. B. Simeral. 2004. Climate monitoring comments: Central Alaska Network Inventory and Monitoring Program. Available from ftp://ftp.wrcc.dri.edu/nps/alaska/cakn/npscakncomments040406.pdf. (accessed 6 April 2004)

Redmond, K. T., D. B. Simeral, and G. D. McCurdy. 2005. Climate monitoring for southwest Alaska national parks: network design and site selection. Report 05-01. Western Regional Climate Center, Reno, Nevada.

Redmond, K. T., and G. D. McCurdy. 2005. Channel Islands National Park: Design considerations for weather and climate monitoring. Report 05-02. Western Regional Climate Center, Reno, Nevada.

Sevruk, B., and W. R. Hamon. 1984. International comparison of national precipitation gauges with a reference pit gauge. Instruments and Observing Methods, Report No 17, WMO/TD – 38, World Meteorological Organization, Geneva, Switzerland.

Simpson, J. J., G. L. Hufford, C. Daly, J. S. Berg, and M. D. Fleming. 2005. Comparing maps of mean monthly surface temperature and precipitation for Alaska and adjacent areas of Canada produced by two different methods. Arctic **58**:137-161.

Whiteman, C. D. 2000. Mountain Meteorology: Fundamentals and Applications. Oxford University Press, Oxford, UK.

Wilson, E. O. 1998. Consilience: The Unity of Knowledge. Knopf, New York.

World Meteorological Organization. 1983. Guide to meteorological instruments and methods of observation, No. 8, 5th edition, World Meteorological Organization, Geneva Switzerland.

World Meteorological Organization. 2005. Organization and planning of intercomparisons of rainfall intensity gauges. World Meteorological Organization, Geneva Switzerland.

Yang, D., B. E. Goodison, J. R. Metcalfe, V. S. Golubev, R. Bates, T. Pangburn, and C. Hanson. 1998. Accuracy of NWS 8" standard nonrecording precipitation gauge: results and application of WMO intercomparison. Journal of Atmospheric and Oceanic Technology **15**:54-68.

Yang, D., B. E. Goodison, J. R. Metcalfe, P. Louie, E. Elomaa, C. Hanson, V. Bolubev, T. Gunther, J. Milkovic, and M. Lapin. 2001. Compatibility evaluation of national precipitation gauge measurements. Journal of Geophysical Research **106**:1481-1491.

Appendix F. Descriptions of weather/climate monitoring networks.

F.1. Clean Air Status and Trends Network (CASTNet)

- Purpose of network: provide information for evaluating the effectiveness of national emission-control strategies.
- Primary management agency: EPA.
- Data Website: http://epa.gov/castnet/.
- Measured weather/climate elements:
  Air temperature.
  Precipitation.
  Relative humidity.
  Wind speed.
  Wind direction.
  Wind gust.
  Gust direction.
  Solar radiation.
  Soil moisture and temperature.
- Sampling frequency: hourly.
- Reporting frequency: hourly.
- Estimated station cost: $13K.
- Network strengths:
  o Data are high quality.
  o Sites are maintained well.
- Network weaknesses:
  o Density of station coverage is low.
  o Shorter periods of record for western United States.

CASTNet primarily is an air-quality-monitoring network managed by the EPA. The elements shown here are intended to support interpretation of measured air-quality parameters such as ozone, nitrates, sulfides, etc., which also are measured at CASTNet sites.

F.2. NWS Cooperative Observer Program (COOP)

- Purpose of network:
  o Provide observational, meteorological data required to define U.S. climate and help measure long-term climate changes.
  o Provide observational, meteorologic data in near real-time to support forecasting and warning mechanisms and other public service programs of the NWS.
- Primary management agency: NOAA (NWS).
- Data Website: data are available from the NCDC (http://www.ncdc.noaa.gov), RCCs (e.g., WRCC, http://www.wrcc.dri.edu), and state climate offices.
- Measured weather/climate elements
  o Maximum, minimum, and observation-time temperature.
  o Precipitation, snowfall, snow depth.

o Pan evaporation (some stations).
- Sampling frequency: daily.
- Reporting frequency: daily or monthly (station-dependent).
- Estimated station cost: $2K with maintenance costs of $500–900/year.
- Network strengths:
  o Decade–century records at most sites.
  o Widespread national coverage (thousands of stations).
  o Excellent data quality when well-maintained.
  o Relatively inexpensive; highly cost effective.
  o Manual measurements; not automated.
- Network weaknesses:
  o Uneven exposures; many are not well-maintained.
  o Dependence on schedules for volunteer observers.
  o Slow entry of data from many stations into national archives.
  o Data subject to observational methodology; not always documented.
  o Manual measurements; not automated and not hourly.

The COOP network has long served as the main climate observation network in the United States. Readings are usually made by volunteers using equipment supplied, installed, and maintained by the federal government. The observer in effect acts as a host for the data-gathering activities and supplies the labor; this is truly a "cooperative" effort. The SAO sites often are considered to be part of the cooperative network as well if they collect the previously mentioned types of weather/climate observations. Typical observation days are morning to morning, evening to evening, or midnight to midnight. By convention, observations are ascribed to the date the instrument was reset at the end of the observational period. For this reason, midnight observations represent the end of a day. The Historical Climate Network is a subset of the cooperative network but contains longer and more complete records.

F.3. NOAA Climate Reference Network (CRN)

- Purpose of network: provide long-term homogeneous measurements of temperature and precipitation that can be coupled with long-term historic observations to monitor present and future climate change.
- Primary management agency: NOAA.
- Data Website: http://www.ncdc.noaa.gov/crn/.
- Measured weather/climate elements:
  o Air temperature (triply redundant, aspirated).
  o Precipitation (three-wire Geonor gauge).
  o Wind speed.
  o Solar radiation.
  o Ground surface temperature.
- Sampling frequency: precipitation can be sampled either 5 or 15 minutes. Temperature sampled every 5 minutes. All other elements sampled every 15 minutes.
- Reporting frequency: hourly or every three hours.
- Estimated station cost: $30K with maintenance costs around $2K/year.
- Network strengths:

o Station siting is excellent (appropriate for long-term climate monitoring).

o Data quality is excellent.

o Site maintenance is excellent.

- Network weaknesses:

o CRN network is still developing.

o Period of record is short compared to other automated networks. Earliest sites date from 2004.

o Station coverage is limited.

o Not intended for snowy climates.

Data from the CRN are used in operational climate-monitoring activities and are used to place current climate patterns into a historic perspective. The CRN is intended as a reference network for the United States that meets the requirements of the Global Climate Observing System. Up to 115 CRN sites are planned for installation, but the actual number of installed sites will depend on available funding.

F.4. Citizen Weather Observer Program (CWOP)

- Purpose of network: collect observations from private citizens and make these data available for homeland security and other weather applications, providing constant feedback to the observers to maintain high data quality.
- Primary management agency: NOAA MADIS program.
- Data Website: http://www.wxqa.com.
- Measured weather/climate elements:

o Air temperature.

o Dewpoint temperature.

o Precipitation.

o Wind speed and direction.

o Barometric Pressure.

- Sampling frequency: 15 minutes or less.
- Reporting frequency: 15 minutes.
- Estimated station cost: unknown.
- Network strengths:

o Active partnership between public agencies and private citizens.

o Large number of participant sites.

o Regular communications between data providers and users, encouraging higher data quality.

- Network weaknesses:

o Variable instrumentation platforms.

o Metadata are sometimes limited.

The CWOP network is a public-private partnership with U.S. citizens and various agencies including NOAA, NASA (National Aeronautics and Space Administration), and various universities. There are over 4500 registered sites worldwide, with close to 3000 of these sites located in North America.

F.5. NPS Gaseous Pollutant Monitoring Program (GPMP)

- Purpose of network: measurement of ozone and related meteorological elements.
- Primary management agency: NPS.
- Data website: http://www2.nature.nps.gov/air/monitoring.
- Measured weather/climate elements:
  o Air temperature.
  o Relative humidity
  o Precipitation.
  o Wind speed and direction.
  o Solar radiation.
  o Surface wetness
- Sampling frequency: continuous.
- Reporting frequency: hourly.
- Estimated station cost: unknown.
- Network strengths:
  o Stations are located within NPS park units.
  o Data quality is excellent, with high data standards.
  o Provides unique measurements that are not available elsewhere.
  o Records are up to 2 decades in length.
  o Site maintenance is excellent.
  o Thermometers are aspirated.
- Network weaknesses:
  o Not easy to download the entire data set or to ingest live data.
  o Period of record is short compared to other automated networks. Earliest sites date from 2004.
  o Station spacing and coverage: station installation is episodic, driven by opportunistic situations.

The NPS web site indicates that there are 33 sites with continuous ozone analysis run by NPS, with records from a few to about 16-17 years. Of these stations, 12 are labeled as GPMP sites and the rest are labeled as CASTNet sites. All of these have standard meteorological measurements, including a 10-m mast. Another 9 GPMP sites are located within NPS units but run by cooperating agencies. A number of other sites (1-2 dozen) ran for differing periods in the past, generally less than 5-10 years.

F.6. The University Center for Atmospheric Research GPS/MET Experiment (GPSMET)

- Purpose of network: use signals from GPS satellites that are occulted by the Earth to demonstrate active limb sounding for the Earth's atmosphere.
- Primary management agency: University Center for Atmospheric Research (UCAR).
- Data website: http://www.cosmic.ucar.edu/gpsmet/.
- Measured weather/climate elements:
  o Air temperature.
  o Relative humidity
  o Pressure.

o Wind speed and direction.
- Sampling frequency: once or twice daily.
- Reporting frequency: once or twice daily.
- Estimated station cost: unknown.
- Network strengths:
  o Can estimate vertical profiles of standard climate elements such as temperature.
  o Satellite-based network: can provide measurements over remote areas such as oceans.
- Network weaknesses:
  o Satellite-based network: this is not a true near-surface observation network, as climate elements are estimated from space.
  o There are only on the order of several hundred points around the world for which GPSMET measurements are made, so station coverage is limited.

The GPSMET network started in the mid-1990s in response to the need to monitor temporal changes in vertical profiles of key climate elements identified by the Committee on Earth and Environmental Sciences Data, such as temperature and humidity. The University Center for Atmospheric Research oversees this network. This is not a surface-based network, so it provides estimates, not actual observations, of near-surface climate elements.

F.7. NOAA Earth Systems Research Laboratory Observatory Operations Group (OBOP)

- Purpose of network: monitor baseline conditions of carbon dioxide and other trace gases in the Earth's atmosphere.
- Primary management agency: NOAA.
- Data website: http://www.cmdl.noaa.gov/obop/.
- Measured weather/climate elements:
  o Air temperature.
  o Precipitation.
  o Pressure.
  o Wind speed and direction.
  o Wind gust.
  o Solar radiation
- Sampling frequency: hourly.
- Reporting frequency: hourly.
- Estimated station cost: unknown.
- Network strengths:
  o Relatively long periods of record.
  o High data quality.
  o Complete metadata
- Network weaknesses:
  o Very few stations.

The NOAA Earth Systems Research Laboratory operates five atmospheric baseline observatories worldwide. These stations monitor atmospheric concentrations of carbon dioxide and other trace gases, with meteorological measurements being conducted in support of this mission. These stations started taking observations in the 1950s or later.

F.8. Remote Automated Weather Station (RAWS)

- Purpose of network: provide near-real-time (hourly or near hourly) measurements of meteorologic variables for use in fire weather forecasts and climatology. Data from RAWS also are used for natural resource management, flood forecasting, natural hazard management, and air-quality monitoring.
- Primary management agency: WRCC, National Interagency Fire Center.
- Data Website: http://www.raws.dri.edu/index.html.
- Measured weather/climate elements:
  o Air temperature.
  o Precipitation.
  o Relative humidity.
  o Wind speed.
  o Wind direction.
  o Wind gust.
  o Gust direction.
  o Solar radiation.
  o Soil moisture and temperature.
- Sampling frequency: 1 or 10 minutes, element-dependent.
- Reporting frequency: generally hourly. Some stations report every 15 or 30 minutes.
- Estimated station cost: $12K with satellite telemetry ($8K without satellite telemetry); maintenance costs are around $2K/year.
- Network strengths:
  o Metadata records are usually complete.
  o Sites are located in remote areas.
  o Sites are generally well-maintained.
  o Entire period of record available on-line.
- Network weaknesses:
  o RAWS network is focused largely on fire management needs (formerly focused only on fire needs).
  o Frozen precipitation is not measured reliably.
  o Station operation is not always continuous.
  o Data transmission is completed via one-way telemetry. Data are therefore recoverable either in real-time or not at all.

The RAWS network is used by many land-management agencies, such as the BLM, NPS, Fish and Wildlife Service, Bureau of Indian Affairs, Forest Service, and other agencies. The RAWS network was one of the first automated weather station networks to be installed in the United States. Most gauges do not have heaters, so hydrologic measurements are of little value when temperatures dip below freezing or reach freezing after snow. There are approximately 1100 real-time sites in this network and about 1800 historic sites (some are decommissioned or moved). The sites can transmit data all winter but may be in deep snow in some locations. The

WRCC is the archive for this network and receives station data and metadata through a special connection to the National Interagency Fire Center in Boise, Idaho.

F.9. NWS/FAA Surface Airways Observation Network (SAO)

- Purpose of network: provide near-real-time (hourly or near hourly) measurements of meteorologic variables and are used both for airport operations and weather forecasting.
- Primary management agency: NOAA, FAA.
- Data Website: data are available from state climate offices, RCCs (e.g., WRCC, http://www.wrcc.dri.edu), and NCDC (http://www.ncdc.noaa.gov).
- Measured weather/climate elements:
  o Air temperature.
  o Dewpoint and/or relative humidity.
  o Wind speed.
  o Wind direction.
  o Wind gust.
  o Gust direction.
  o Barometric pressure.
  o Precipitation (not at many FAA sites).
  o Sky cover.
  o Ceiling (cloud height).
  o Visibility.
- Sampling frequency: element-dependent.
- Reporting frequency: element-dependent.
- Estimated station cost: $100–$200K with maintenance costs approximately $10K/year.
- Network strengths:
  o Records generally extend over several decades.
  o Consistent maintenance and station operations.
  o Data record is reasonably complete and usually high quality.
  o Hourly or sub-hourly data.
- Network weaknesses:
  o Nearly all sites are located at airports.
  o Data quality can be related to size of airport—smaller airports tend to have poorer datasets.
  o Influences from urbanization and other land-use changes.

These stations are managed by NOAA, U. S. Navy, U. S. Air Force, and FAA. These stations are located generally at major airports and military bases. The FAA stations often do not record precipitation, or they provide precipitation records of reduced quality. Automated stations are typically ASOSs for the NWS or AWOSs for the FAA. Some sites only report episodically with observers paid per observation.

Appendix G. Electronic supplements.

G.1 ACIS metadata file for weather and climate stations associated with the PACN:
http://www.wrcc.dri.edu/nps/pub/pacn/metadata/PACN_from_ACIS.tar.gz.

G.2 PACN metadata files for weather and climate stations associated with the PACN:
http://www.wrcc.dri.edu/nps/pub/pacn/metadata/PACN_NPS.tar.gz.

Appendix H. Additional weather/climate stations.

Name	Lat.	Lon.	Elev. (m)	Network	Start	End
Nene Nest	20.741	-156.249	790	HaleNet	3/1990	Present
Pu'u Pahu	20.761	-156.280	500	HaleNet	6/1998	Present
Haleakala National Park HQ	20.763	-156.251	646	HaleNet	6/1998	Present
Summit	20.714	-156.259	912	HaleNet	4/1990	Present
Auwahi	20.648	-156.345	378	HaleNet	12/2000	Present
Waikamoi	20.777	-156.225	598	HaleNet	8/2001	Present
Pohaku Palaha	20.734	-156.143	750	HaleNet	6/1992	Present
Treeline	20.737	-156.127	689	HaleNet	6/1992	Present
Horseshoe Pu'u	20.738	-156.111	588	HaleNet	6/1992	11/1996
Big Bog	20.730	-156.095	503	HaleNet	6/1992	Present
Kula Ag. Exp. Station	20.761	-156.323	293	HaleNet	6/1998	Present
Kealakomo	19.295	-155.144	88	NFDRS	1/1/1995	Present
Kalpan	19.317	-155.667	9	NFDRS	10/13/1980	5/28/1998
Umatac	13.291	144.660	17	USGS	12/1978	Present
Windward Hills	13.376	144.739	34	USGS	2/1974	Present
Mount Chachao	13.438	144.709	77	USGS	2/1973	Present
Dededo	13.517	144.847	35	USGS	3/1987	Present
Fena Dam	13.359	144.706	0	USGS	M	M
Almagosa	13.351	144.681	0	USGS	M	M
Mt. Jumullong Manglo	13.323	144.670	68	USGS	M	M
Andersen AFB	13.575	144.929	50	USGS	M	M
Mt. Santa Rosa	13.536	144.865	77	USGS	M	M

NPS/PACN/NRTR—2006/003, August 2006